MY TIME WITH ANTONIONI

by the same author

EMOTION PICTURES
THE LOGIC OF IMAGES
THE ACT OF SEEING

My Time with Antonioni

The Diary of an Extraordinary Experience

WIM WENDERS

translated by MICHAEL HOFMANN

ff
faber and faber
LONDON·NEW YORK

First published in Germany in 1995
by Verlag der Autoren, Frankfurt am Main

First published in the United Kingdom in 2000
by Faber and Faber Limited
3 Queen Square London WC1N 3AU
Published in the United States by Faber Inc.,
an affiliate of Farrar, Straus, Giroux, New York

Photoset by Parker Typesetting Service, Leicester
Printed in England by Clays Ltd, St Ives plc

All rights reserved

© Verlag der Autoren, 1995
translation © Michael Hofmann, 2000
photographs © Donata Wenders

Wim Wenders is hereby identified as author of this
work in accordance with Section 77 of the Copyright,
Designs and Patents Act 1988

*This book is sold subject to the condition that it shall not, by way
of trade or otherwise, be lent, resold, hired out or otherwise circulated
without the publisher's prior consent in any form of binding or cover other
than that in which it is published and without a similar condition including
this condition being imposed on the subsequent purchaser*

A CIP record for this book
is available from the British Library

ISBN 0–571–20076–1

For Enrica, Andrea, Tonino, and all the others . . .

The Protagonists
Behind the camera

MICHELANGELO: Michelangelo Antonioni, film director
ENRICA: Enrica Antonioni, his wife. She worked for many years as his assistant. She plays the 'boutique owner'
TONINO: Tonino Guerra, poet and screenwriter. The author of numerous film scripts for Antonioni, Fellini, Tarkovsky, Angelopoulos, etc.
ALFIO: Alfio Contini, cameraman
PINO: Giuseppe Venditi, assistant cameraman
ANDREA: Dr Andrea Boni, Antonioni's personal assistant
CLAUDIO: Claudio di Mauro, editor
'I': Wim Wenders, film director
DONATA: Donata Wenders, his wife. Camerawoman and photographer
ROBBY: Robby Müller, cameraman
BEATRICE: Beatrice Banfi, first assistant director
THIERRY: Thierry Flamand, set designer and film architect
ESTHER: Esther Walz, costume designer
ARUNA: continuity
JOLANDA: Jolanda Darbyshire, Wenders' personal assistant
PETER: Peter Przygodda, editor
PHILIPPE: Philippe Carcassonne, producer
STEPHANE: Stephane Tchalgadjieff, producer
ULI: Uli Felsberg, producer, runs Road Movies, Wenders' production company
FELICE: Felice Laudadio, film journalist, festival organizer and producer
JEAN-PIERRE: Jean-Pierre Ruh, sound recordist
GIANCARLO: stage manager

In front of the camera

JOHN: John Malkovich – 'the director'
SOPHIE: Sophie Marceau – young woman in Portofino
KIM: Kim Rossi-Stuart – Silvano
INES: Ines Sastre – Carmen
IRENE: Irene Jacob – young woman in Aix
VINCENT: Vincent Perez – Niccolo, the young man
JEAN: Jean Reno – Carlo
FANNY: Fanny Ardant – Patrizia
PETER: Peter Weller – Roberto
CHIARA: Chiara Caselli – Olga
MARCELLO: Marcello Mastroianni – the schoolteacher, fisherman, painter, businessman
EVA: Eva Mattes – fisherman's daughter
JEANNE: Jeanne Moreau – traveller

Prologue

I first met Michelangelo Antonioni in 1982 in Cannes, where he was showing his film *Identificazione di una donna*. I had brought *Hammett* to the film festival, and was as impressed with Antonioni's new film as I had been by *Blow-Up* or *Zabriskie Point* or, before that, by *L'Avventura*, *La Notte* or *L'Eclisse*.

As part of a documentary I was making on the development of film language, I had invited all the directors present at Cannes to speak to camera on the future of the cinema as they saw it. Many of them had taken up my invitation, among them Werner Herzog, Rainer Fassbinder, Steven Spielberg, Jean-Luc Godard and – Antonioni. Each director was left by himself in a room with a Nagra tape-recorder, a 16 mm camera and some brief instructions. Each was free to 'direct' his reply to the question I put to them all; they could be brief, or if they liked they could use up the whole reel of film, roughly ten minutes. The finished film was called *Chambre 666*, after the room in the Hotel Martinez where it had all taken place. It was the last available hotel room in the whole of Cannes.

For me, the most impressive statement on the future of the cinema was that of Michelangelo Antonioni, which is why it went into the film completely unedited, including the moment when Michelangelo had finished speaking, and walked over to the camera to switch it off.

What he said was this:

It's true, film is in grave danger. But we shouldn't overlook other aspects of the problem. The effect of TV on people's viewing habits and expectations – especially children's – is clear. On the other hand, we can't deny that part of the reason that the situation seems so grave to us is because we belong to an older generation. What we should do is try to adapt to the different visual technologies that are coming into being.

New forms of reproduction such as magnetic tape will probably come to replace traditional film stock, which no longer meets our needs. Scorsese has already pointed out that some older colour films have begun to fade. The problem of entertaining ever-larger numbers of people may be solved by electronics, by lasers, or by other technologies still to be discovered – who can say?

Of course, I'm just as worried as anyone else about the future of the cinema as we know it. We're attached to it because it gave us so many ways of saying what we felt and thought we had to say. But as the spectrum of new technical possibilities gets wider, that feeling will eventually disappear. There probably always was that discrepancy between the present and the unimaginable future. Who knows what houses are going to look like in future – the structures we see when we look out of the window probably won't even exist tomorrow. We shouldn't think of the immediate future either, but of the distant future; we must concern ourselves with the kind of world that a future race of humans will inhabit.

I'm not such a pessimist. I've always been someone who tried to adapt to whatever forms of expression coped best with the contemporary world. I've used video on one of my films; I've experimented with colour, and I've painted reality. The technique was crude, but it represented some kind of advance. I want to go on experimenting, because I believe that the possibilities of video will give us a different sense of ourselves.

It's not an easy thing, to talk about the future of the cinema. High-definition video cassettes will soon bring it into our houses; cinemas probably won't be needed any more. All our contemporary structures will disappear. It won't be quick or straightforward, but it will happen, and we can't do anything to prevent it. All we can do is try to adjust to it.

Already in *Deserto rosso*, I was looking at the question of adapting – adapting to new technologies, to the polluted air we'll probably have to breathe. Even our physical bodies will probably evolve – who can say in what ways. The future will probably present itself with a ruthlessness we can't yet imagine. I'm only going to repeat myself now; I'm not a philosopher or a speech-maker. I'd rather work and try things out than talk about it. My sense is: it won't be all that hard to turn us into new people, better used to dealing with the new technologies.

It wasn't just the statement that impressed me, it was Antonioni himself – his confident yet unassuming way of talking, his movements, the way he walked up and down in front of the camera, and stood by the window. The man was as cool and stylish as his work, and his outlook was every bit as radical and modern as the films he made.

Barely a year after our meeting, I heard that he had suffered a stroke which had left him aphasic, severely limited in his ability to speak. It was upsetting news, and I could only hope that rehabilitation and further treatment might improve his condition. But I lost touch with Antonioni until, a couple of years later, I was approached by a producer who asked whether I would be prepared to step in for Antonioni as a back-up director, because without someone else, no film of his would find insurers.

So I met up with Michelangelo again in Rome, and for a time it looked as though the project – called 'Due telegrammi', based on one of Antonioni's own stories and with a script by Rudi Wurlitzer – was going to happen. But there were delays due to financial and casting problems, and finally I couldn't keep myself available for it any longer because my own project, *Until the End of the World*, got under way. I disappeared into that for several years, and once more lost touch with Michelangelo.

Then, in autumn 1993, I was approached by another producer, Stéphane Tchalgadjieff, to see if I would do something similar. Tchalgadjieff, a French producer born in Armenia, was known to me principally as the producer of some of Jacques Rivette's early films. The project he was developing with Michelangelo was called *Par delà des Nuages*, and was based on several stories from Antonioni's book, *Quel bowling sul Tevere* (The Bowling Alley on the Tiber), which I'd read once years ago, and which is also where the story for 'Due telegrammi' had come from. The stories had been given a framing narrative about a film director – evidently not a million miles from Antonioni himself – and Tchalgadjieff was looking not only for a back-up director to satisfy the insurance companies, in view of Antonioni's continuing disability, but also for a co-director, who was to direct the framing narrative around the individual episodes, which of course would be directed by Antonioni himself.

By then I had finished *Faraway, So Close*, and I didn't have another project that was ready to go. I went to see Michelangelo again in Rome and he made it clear to me that I was his choice and that he wanted me to be involved, so I agreed. It obviously required a different measure of participation than the earlier project, but that made it more realistic. In addition to my personal sympathy for Michelangelo, and my admiration for his work, there was one particularly strong reason why I wanted to embark on this extraordinary venture: I was completely convinced that a director like Antonioni, in spite of his age and his handicap, should be given an opportunity to make the film he could clearly see in his mind's eye. That someone of his calibre should be barred from making a film just because he could no longer speak seemed to me completely unacceptable.

It was obvious that he could understand everything that was put to him, and that mentally he was as alert as ever. He hadn't lost his sense of humour either; it was just that he couldn't speak, except for a dozen or so words of basic Italian, things like *si* and *no*, *ciao*, *doppo*, *via*, *fuori*, *domani*, *andiamo*, *vino* and *mangiare*. I remember one of our first meetings, in a restaurant in Rome. His wife Enrica, who always interprets for him, had just popped out. Antonioni and I sat in silence for a moment, and I suppose I said something to him in French, which, along with my poor Italian, was how I used to communicate with him during the filming. He shrugged his shoulders, smiled sadly and said just one word, 'Parlare!', while at the same time waving his hand back and forth in front of his face, with the tips of fingers and thumb held together – the inimitable gesture that will always be part of the way I remember him.

Antonioni's stroke had destroyed the letter-forming and spelling centres of his brain, so he was unable to write or speak. As the stroke had affected his right side, he could draw only with his left hand. And that was what he did as a last resort when trying to make his meaning clear to us, if Enrica's truly amazing knack of finding the words he wanted had for once failed her. And then Enrica, or Michelangelo's personal assistant Andrea Boni, would always have a pad and pencil handy, so that he could make a sketch to clarify his meaning. These left-handed sketches of his were amazingly precise for a right-hander, and became an indispensable means of communication, especially once the actual filming had begun.

From the outset I was astonished by the way Michelangelo was reconciled to his handicap, and by the patience he always showed towards other people until they finally understood him. If all our guesses and various suggestions failed to hit the nail on the head, and we just couldn't grasp what he was trying to tell us, he did not despair but started to laugh and tap his finger against his brow, as if to say, 'What a lot of idiots you are!' And in the end someone would get the point of a drawing or a gesture that had long eluded us.

Even though Michelangelo was unable to write himself, he was well able to correct or edit something someone else had written. And thank God there was someone at hand who wrote in such a way that he felt understood from the outset: Tonino Guerra, his screenwriter.

Tonino and Michelangelo were old friends and had written a lot of films together, beginning with *L'Avventura* (1959). The scenes that Tonino had scripted were based on Antonioni's own stories in *Quel bowling sul Tevere*, published in 1983, a collection of short stories, never-used ideas for films, diary entries, essays, aphorisms and scraps of dialogue.

With the help of Enrica and Andrea, Michelangelo, Tonino and I went through all these stories again, before finally settling on four of them for the film. They were 'Cronaca di un amore mai esistito' (The Story of a Love that Never Was), 'La ragazza, il delitto' (The Girl and the Crime), 'Questo corpo di fango' (This Filthy Body), and finally 'Due telegrammi' ('Two Telegrams'), which we updated to 'Due telefaxi'.

All four were love stories, though in each case it was a different and unrealizable kind of love.

'Cronaca di un amore mai esistito' is set in Antonioni's home town of Ferrara, a wealthy old industrial and university town in the north of Italy. Travelling through the town, a young man called Silvano meets a young woman, Carmen, who teaches in a school in a nearby village. For one night he finds himself staying in the same hotel as her. The two of them fall in love with each other right away; they go for a long walk together, feeling that the relationship was predestined. After a long kiss, it seems inevitable that they will indeed spend the night together. But then Silvano – through pride, exhaustion or some other reason – doesn't visit her in her room, and instead falls asleep in his clothes on his own bed. When he wakes up the following morning, Carmen has already left for work.

Silvano, too, goes on his way, and they don't see each other again, though clearly they remain intensely involved with each other emotionally. Then, two or three years later, they run into one another in a cinema. This time they go straight back to Carmen's house, talk, take off their clothes, and are about to make love when Silvano suddenly gets up, puts his clothes on, and leaves Carmen without any explanation, in order, as he later admits to himself, 'not to disturb a desire' he has learned to live with and perhaps depend on. They never see each other again, though in their minds they will always remain inseparable.

'La ragazza, il delitto' is set in Portofino, a little harbour town on the Italian Riviera not far from Genoa. A man – a film director – is on the lookout for a story. His eye is caught by a young woman working as a sales assistant in a harbourfront boutique. He's strangely fascinated by her eyes and her manner, which are those of a character he's been thinking of. The woman suddenly turns to him and tells him her story: she killed her father, stabbing him twelve times with a knife, after which she was arrested and ultimately acquitted in court. The two of them enjoy a night of love, then go their separate ways. The woman had got too close to the director for him to be able to pursue her story.

'Questo corpo di fango', set in an anonymous city, is about a young man, Niccolo, who happens to meet a young woman on her way to church. He starts flirting with her, and ends up accompanying her all the way to the church. He goes in with her and watches her at her devotions. Then he falls asleep, and when he wakes up the church is empty. He dashes out, runs back the same way, and he sees the girl again. The two of them resume their conversation, with greater earnestness now. Niccolo is terribly moved by the girl, and his feeling for her grows deeper and stronger, to the point where he realizes he wants to spend the rest of his life with her. Standing at her door, he asks if he can see her tomorrow. She replies: 'Tomorrow I'm entering a convent.' Niccolo's life is shattered.

'Due telefaxi' is the story of a businesswoman, Catherine, who works in a stylish office near the top of a modern office block. She gets a fax from her husband, asking her for a divorce. Catherine is completely distraught. For a while she drives aimlessly through the city, then she returns to her office, but she can't concentrate on her work. Evening comes and people start going home. That night Catherine stares out of the window for hours, finally focusing her attention on a man who's still working in an office in the building opposite. Their offices are the only ones still lit up in their respective buildings, high above the city. Catherine sends the unknown businessman a fax, asking him to help her. He spots the woman who's been observing him, and throws her fax out of the window. Catherine won't accept this rejection, and she manages to find her way up to his office, where the pair of them are finally left in a breathless confrontation.

With Tonino's help I drafted a new framing story that had the character of the 'director' developed in a different way to that envisaged by the producer. I thought he should be more fictionalized, not so obviously 'Antonioni', and that Michelangelo shouldn't play the part himself either. A previous version of the script had suggested that, but Antonioni was very emphatic about not wanting to be the protagonist in his own film. He would only consider appearing in it if the project couldn't be made otherwise. He insisted that the part needed a younger actor, even though we wanted to keep as many of his own thoughts as we could, for the character's 'inner voice'. Enrica made Michelangelo's personal archive available to us – an inexhaustible reservoir of notes, aphorisms and ideas that he'd jotted down over the years. Enrica and Michelangelo selected some of those that seemed relevant to our film. So the inner voice in my 'framework', as we called it, was completely founded on texts by Antonioni himself, even though the 'director' was no longer physically or psychologically to be identified with 'Michelangelo'.

Because of this, I did not want the four episodes to have the status of 'visions' or 'dreams' or any other kind of 'fantasies' on the part of the 'director' in the framing narrative, and so I argued for a melding of my part and Antonioni's. He wouldn't consider that, though, and insisted on keeping the four stories separate and self-contained, so that my framework would merely be the bridge between them. I, of course, agreed to that, even though I continued to believe that a melding of the different parts would make for a more interesting film. I didn't want to be assertive in any way, and my first concern was always that Michelangelo should make *his* film.

Antonioni had accepted that I was to shoot the narrative framework, but I think his acceptance may have been rather halfhearted. Certainly, I couldn't help thinking from the start that he tended to see my contribution as something of a 'necessary evil', and that he would rather have shot the whole film by himself. I couldn't blame him for that, after all, I understood his point of view very well. According to the producers, though, the film could not have been financed purely as a four-chapter film, only as a film by Antonioni *and* Wenders together: Antonioni contributing four episodes, and Wenders the framing narrative. And that, finally, is how the film was financed, as a French/German/Italian co-production.

All this needs to be spelled out, because I would gladly have accommodated Michelangelo's more or less evident desire that the film be all *his*, and for a while I tried to keep that open as an option for the producers. But in the end, that would have meant the project collapsing again. The distributors and the TV companies, who had stumped up the money on the basis of advance sales, wanted a film from the two of us. There was no going back on that, for either of us.

It was decided that Michelangelo would film his four episodes first, and after a short break – which would be essential from an organizational point of view – I would shoot my part. Each individual shoot was to last a fortnight, which meant a total time of ten weeks. The budget wouldn't stretch to a single day more.

Antonioni would film his stories using Alfio Contini – his cameraman on *Zabriskie Point* – and I would probably work with Robby Müller, if he was available. That wasn't entirely certain, and it also depended on when filming began. We had originally planned to start in spring 1994, but spring came and the financing and other arrangements were still far from complete. And so the beginning of filming was put back to late summer 1994.

I used the unexpected postponement to shoot, very spontaneously, a little film in Portugal called *Lisbon Story*. That took just five weeks to shoot, and in June I was already back on the case with Michelangelo. Stephane Tchalgadjieff had come up with a very able and flexible co-producer, Philippe Carcassonne, with whom he was now splitting the important French end of the co-production. With Philippe's help, the project was soon so solid that we could ink in a new start date for the shoot: early November in Portofino, the 'La ragazza, il delitto' episode, with Sophie Marceau and John Malkovich as the two leads. Then we would move on to Ferrara, Michelangelo's birthplace, and do the 'Cronaca di un amore mai esistito' episode, with Ines Sastre and Kim Rossi-Stuart. From there we would relocate to Aix-en-Provence and film 'Questo corpo di fango', with Irene Jacob and Vincent Perez, and finish up in Paris for technically the most demanding episode, 'Due telefaxi', in which Fanny Ardant and Jeremy Irons were pencilled in for the leads. If everything went according to plan, Michelangelo would be finished just before Christmas, and I could begin on my part of the shoot in mid-January.

If . . . if . . . In fact, anything was possible, and there was no knowing what would happen. Between my hope that Antonioni would have his shoot completely under control, and direct the whole thing by himself, and the worst-case scenario – that he quite simply couldn't, and that I would be required by the producers and insurers to step into the breach – there were all sorts of possible shadings. On occasion I was pretty much the only optimist around, and it was a struggle to remain optimistic, not least when it became clear that Michelangelo's memory was faulty, and you couldn't be sure from one day to the next whether a decision taken the day before still stood or not. So it seemed crucial to the success of the film, and for Michelangelo's ability to control events, that we plan the shoot in as much detail as possible, and do it in chronological order. The chances of making up for some slip of memory would be much improved if we were able to go forward scene by scene and shot by shot. Beatrice Banfi, Michelangelo's first assistant, had drawn up her schedule accordingly.

The preparations went ahead. Michelangelo did his location recces pretty much by himself, though I often joined him. (It was particularly important that he choose his own locations, because all his films show such an unerring sense of architecture and landscape.) He also did the casting on his own, with Enrica's collaboration. In Alfio Contini he had a cameraman whom he trusted. Of my associates we had Thierry Flamand as chief set designer, and Esther Walz as costume designer.

We all embarked on our adventure with an equal measure of patience and enthusiasm. The only way to see what sort of film Antonioni had in mind was to let him make it. Therefore, it had to be made.

At last, the shoot: Wenders and Antonioni get to work

THURSDAY 3.11.94   First day of shoot

At last. Because the shoot has been put back from spring to summer and now to autumn, I've been able to be with Michelangelo and the crew during the last week of preparations in Portofino, the location for the first episode, 'La ragazza, il delitto', but on the very eve of the shoot I have to be in Paris to honour a longstanding commitment. The French edition of my book *Once** is coming out, and there's an exhibition in the FNAC, press-conference and interviews, and the whole thing is due to end so late there's no chance of getting back to Italy the same night.

There was a lovely, unexpected ending to the day when we were driven back to the hotel by Martine and Henri Cartier-Bresson. How attentive, kindly and alert the old gentleman was, always so careful not to appear 'old': he'd rather hold open a door himself than have it held open for him.

Yesterday morning we went to see a demonstration of the latest

* A collection of photographs and short stories.

I

HDTV-to-film transfer from Thomson's, who are interested in working with Michelangelo and me. The images on screen, recorded digitally and then put on film, are really impressive, and only barely distinguishable from real film images. That might actually be the perfect language for Michelangelo to shoot his final episode, 'Due telefaxi'. The electronic medium would match the atmosphere of the story. And wouldn't it be appropriate, too, for Michelangelo to make the last part of his last film using the technology of the next century, seeing as he was one of the very first directors with a positive attitude to video, and was never shy of new technology? I agree with the producers that we should present it to Michelangelo, and let him decide if he wants it. I'm less sure whether I should use it for my own shoot. Donata, my wife, is very much against. I'm tempted to, but at the same time I'm afraid the Ferrara fogs will appear too cool, and the lonely figure of the 'director' wouldn't have the same aura and intensity as it would on black and white film. Not that I've quite decided whether to go for black and white or not. I'm not even sure who the cameraman will be. As we're not sure when I'm going to begin, we need to keep our options open, I'm afraid. What's definite is that Robby Müller is shooting Lars von Trier's new film in the spring.

Today, then, the first day of the shoot, Donata and I got up bright and early, took the first plane from Paris to Milan, and drove to Portofino through mist and occasional rain, afraid the weather might make us late. But we arrive on time. The first clapboard is an hour later. The rain has delayed everything, and indeed it will dominate the day's events.

First off, big excitement, not least among the producers: it appears that the moment he got on set, Michelangelo announced that everything is being changed around, so it's not John Malkovich who's going to come out the door and walk down into the town, but Sophie Marceau. That means changing the bedroom, where we're going to film later, from a 'man's room' to a woman's. 'Here we go . . .' you can see the producers thinking. But on closer inspection, the change makes sense.

Michelangelo just hadn't been in a position before to clear up our misunderstanding. It often seemed to me in our discussions that it was simply too much of an effort for him to make his intentions clear to us, and so he occasionally left us under some misapprehension, fully knowing that the moment of truth would dawn once we were filming. Also, Michelangelo has trouble differentiating between 'he' and 'she' when speaking, so we were often uncertain whether he was talking about the male or the female character in a story. But now, on set, everything has become clear. It is John who will walk down the hill, and see Sophie just opening her door. Their eyes will meet and she will hurry off, John following her.

Michelangelo has a couple of cameras set up in the narrow lane, and is sitting squeezed behind a pair of monitors. What had seemed likely during the pre-production meetings now turns out to be the case: he's used to filming this way, with two cameras at once. It doesn't even occur to him any more to direct two separate set-ups. I'm torn what to think about it. The two cameras might get in each other's way: it won't be possible for them both to frame ideally, and cutting between them might be 'jumpy'. Then again, if Antonioni has always worked like that, it's certainly pointless to suggest anything else – after all, he's made fantastic films using this method. Alfio Contini is muttering that he's not too thrilled about it either, but that's Antonioni for you. In *Zabriskie Point* he'd used two cameras the whole time as well.

Unquestionably, it's a technique that makes for greater distance from the characters: the narrator's point of view isn't that of the actors. It's purely Michelangelo's point of view; he's standing alongside the characters, not identifying with them at all. No wonder, I conclude, after analysing the whole thing with Donata, that this two-camera technique is getting to me: what I've always done in my films is empathize with my characters. Michelangelo's point of view is considerably cooler, which isn't to say that it's necessarily 'dispassionate'. What his cameras show doesn't tally with any one individual's eye, but represents an 'objective view'. And that's also the only way I have of justifying to myself

Michelangelo's liberal use of the zoom lens. That piece of equipment really is my *bête noire*, because it doesn't correspond to the vision of a human eye; it's an artificial vision. Human beings need to go up to something to see it closely, and the way you do that with a camera is to move it up. You can't make a thing 'zoom' into close-up just with your eye. But Michelangelo seems to have no such hang-ups. I avoid any aesthetic debate. It's his film we're shooting here, not mine.

Except that we're not shooting much of anything just now. The rain is getting heavier, and after lunch the cameras are set up for the next shot, but there's no more filming. The little lane we wanted to film in is like a mountain stream. Everybody's philosophical about it, especially John and Sophie.

During the break, I hear of some more excitement last night. Sophie was seriously considering pulling out, because she thought her part had gone through changes she didn't approve of. I can see her point. During the final rewrites her first and last lines were changed, and her whole part seemed to be suspended between them. We talk about it with Tonino later, and decide to work on Michelangelo. The original version of the last sentence is: 'I don't remember . . .' and that's really much better than all the subsequent ideas. I have a word with Sophie, promise to do my best to get the line reinstated, and hope she gets her confidence back for the rest of the shoot.

Everyone feels calmer in the evening, even the producers, in spite of the fact that so little was shot, because Michelangelo has clearly shown that he's capable of doing his job. A real jolt went through him today: he stood upright, and his expression radiated pride and energy. Only two days ago, when we flew to Paris, I was seriously worried. I was even afraid that Michelangelo might have a crisis at the beginning of the shoot, because the realization of his long-held dream would be too much for him. Today he's convinced us of the opposite.

Much of the credit for the fact that the film is really going ahead surely belongs with Enrica. For ten years, through all kinds of ups and downs, she's believed in it and fought for it.

Having this huge crew and these actors assembled here – all of us ready to give everything we have over the coming weeks – to make a film out of this shooting script and this schedule is Enrica's personal triumph. And today, on the first day of the shoot, there she is standing in front of the monitors next to Michelangelo, beaming all over her face. Of course everyone is making a fuss of him, but we know that Enrica was and is the driving force behind him. A great dream is becoming reality, for both of them. Now it is up to us to sustain the dream to the end, so there is no rude awakening.

In looking for my own niche, I keep in the background, and leave various initiatives and suggestions with Michelangelo's helpers, Beatrice, Andrea or Alfio Contini. I will have succeeded in my task if I find the right balance between staying out of it and, where absolutely necessary, taking a hand. And above all, I need to learn to keep my own ideas on how I would shoot a scene to myself, because they're not helpful in this situation.

The little documentary crew, with Agnes Godard as camerawoman, shooting colour footage with a digital Betacam and black and white on Super-8, are also trying to get the measure of their job. Enrica is in charge of this film-within-a-film, but she's so much in demand as an interpreter for Michelangelo that she is far more involved in the shoot than in her documentary-maker's role. That, too, will take a while to find its level. For now, we all need to be patient.

What worries me more tonight is our producers. Philippe Carcassonne, hitherto a tower of strength, seems noticeably gloomy and pessimistic. I hope he recovers himself.

I take a few stills photographs, with the Fuji 6 × 9, rather sheepishly. Donata dusts off her new Nikon F4 and takes some pictures of the shoot and the crew, in black and white. I'm sticking to colour.

It's very late, and I feel totally exhausted. Being at a shoot without being in charge is much more taxing than I had imagined.

Over supper, we laughed till we cried while Tonino regaled us with the story of how Fellini was the first person who managed

Tonino Guerra takes shelter from the storm

to get food stains on his back while eating. Tonino demonstrated how Fellini broke a roll in half, and a piece of mortadella flew up in the air and landed between his shoulderblades. He kept imitating Fellini standing there, with the slice of meat sticking to his back, worrying about how cross Giulietta would be when she'd get to hear about his foolish adventure.

Friday 4.11.94   Second day of shoot

Afternoon. On location in a little boutique on the waterfront at Portofino. I was able to nab one of the changing rooms, and have so far been able to defend it successfully; it's the only place that doesn't have a camera in it, or some lights hidden in it. The place is terribly cramped, and everyone keeps treading on each other's toes. All of us, me included, are still looking for our place in this orchestra. In the pandemonium of this tiny boutique, which has got lighting men, set designers, camera assistants, production managers, stagehands and sound recordists swarming all over it, it's like everyone is still tuning their instruments. Everyone wants to please Michelangelo, but despite all this respect and obedience they aren't able to produce harmony: it's still just a loud noise. Lots of people still don't know each other by name; Italian, French and German views of the filming are still divergent and keep colliding the whole time. However, I have made out one pillar of strength and calm in all this, and that's Giancarlo, the Italian stage manager, who's quite unflappable, and has an infectious cheerfulness about him too.

In the morning we were filming in front of the boutique. Sophie as the sales assistant, and Enrica playing the manageress, arrive, open the boutique, and pull up the shutters. John strolls by, turns and sees Sophie kneeling in the window, laying out clothes in the display. I think the first shot came out especially well. The sky was overcast, but the rain held off. The tide was very high in the bay, and little waves kept spilling over the narrow harbourfront. Sophie and John looked at each other silently for a moment, then John walked into the shop.

Malkovich's eye is drawn to something in the window of Armani . . .

. . . or rather, to someone: Sophie Marceau

My fears of yesterday are confirmed: Michelangelo uses the zoom lens in almost every shot; he seems to have no inhibition about employing it time after time after time. One shot, which begins inside on Sophie, and then zooms out till we see John standing outside in front of the window, really makes me wonder. Because the camera's fixed, there's no movement or pan that might disguise the zoom, which is thus instantly identifiable, and strikes me as terribly abrupt. At the same time, though, Michelangelo directs the rest of the scene so fluently and originally, using the zoom, that I feel my aesthetic cavil is inappropriate. It must just be in his blood to shoot like that.

Once, Michelangelo loses his temper with all of us – I mean with Beatrice his assistant, Aruna the continuity girl, and with Alfio and me, when we try to persuade him that John has to walk into shot from the left. Michelangelo wants him from the right, because it makes for a better shot. But the previous shot ended with John walking out of frame on the right. How's he going to edit, if John comes in from the right? Michelangelo is stubborn, and insists on having it his way. He's not interested in our objections about 'crossing the line'. On another occasion, he insists that Sophie looks at John to the right of the camera, while John himself had also looked right. When that's edited, the two of them will be looking straight past each other. Michelangelo keeps looking at the close-up of John on the monitor, where you might think he's actually looking to the left of the camera. Our whole argument is invalidated by the fact that John has a slight squint. You could swear that he's looking to the left of the camera with one eye, and to the right with the other. All our 'sight lines' become somewhat theoretical. At any rate, Michelangelo refuses to be persuaded that Sophie should look left of camera. After a lot of argy-bargy, we reach a compromise whereby Sophie looks right *at* the camera. And that at least *will* edit.

In the afternoon Michelangelo rehearses the main part of the boutique scene, leaving out a lot of what's in the script. I'm not entirely sure whether he's changed his mind, or has just forgotten bits of it. In the script it was a very long scene, with several sections of voice-over. The way it is now, there won't be any room for that. On the other hand, it is a more effective scene. Michelangelo seems less interested in the man's part, which in the book is clearly the dominant one, and more interested in Sophie, which brings the two roles into equilibrium. He keeps telling Sophie he wants her to be more agitated. 'Forte!' is the word he uses. And then with his body language he shows her that she's still too placid, and he sees her as being in greater turmoil.

Until now he's rehearsed the scene and set it up as a master – in other words, right through, without a cut. Again, I ask myself whether he's got the next shot ready in the back of his mind or not? Will he add some close-ups? We're all in the dark, and when we ask him what he's going to do next, he always replies with a gesture that indicates: 'Just leave me to get on with this in peace, and then we'll see.' Or else he says: 'Dopo!' I don't get the sense that he's thinking in terms of the mechanism of different shots that need to be taken *in succession*. Hence the two cameras, so that the edits will be done, as it were, *in parallel*. Michelangelo doesn't think in terms of edits, I'm gradually coming to realize. He thinks within each shot as it happens – or each group of shots, when he's filming with several cameras at once. And only then, after that span of time has been filmed, does he decide how he's going to deal with the next bit. He doesn't design that space–time continuum known as film in advance, the way an architect first designs a house and then builds it; he slowly piles stone on top of stone, allowing himself to be guided more by the feel of a scene than by any predetermined plan. And in the end, in this intuitive and empirical fashion, a surprisingly complicated building is assembled, one that may be more open to its inhabitants – and also to those who see it – than a pre-designed one.

Looking back on it, I remember how rare shot/countershot sequences are in his films in general, and how Michelangelo has always conducted us through his stories with long, complicated camera movements.

Reading through this again just now, I feel a little less certain.

Maybe Michelangelo does 'see' each scene in advance, and maybe he does have an exact sense of it, more than just a shot at a time, only he's not able to tell us what it is. I remember how Enrica said he hardly slept at nights, because he was always thinking of the next scene. If Michelangelo really knew what he wanted, it would make it all the more astonishing if he opened himself to the location, the actors and the scene each morning.

Well, I have now been expelled from my 'office': they needed 'my' changing room for the second camera. Tonino just came by for another discussion of the dialogue and the ending of 'Due telefaxi'. It's so difficult to put his poetic Italian into English. I can really only guess what it must be like in the original. The English versions of his dialogues are sometimes impossible for an actor to say. I wish we had an English writer here, with a good command of Italian. I'm wondering whether I shouldn't write to Sam Shepard after all. He offered to help, and he knows Michelangelo well. He wrote the script for *Zabriskie Point* – on which our Alfio Contini was the cameraman.

Later. Thunder and lightning. It ended up being even wetter than yesterday. In spite of that we managed three shots this morning so, with a bit of luck, we ought to finish the boutique tomorrow. A couple of takes of the master interior, and then we can call it a day, to begin again tomorrow.

Michelangelo is unhappy about something, and we don't really know what. He doesn't seem to like the improvised dialogue between Enrica and Sophie. We assume Tonino will have to come up with a new draft, but later on, back in the hotel, we realize that Michelangelo doesn't want any lines at all; the little scene between the manageress and the assistant is to remain silent, so that the conversation between Sophie and John will be the only speech in the whole episode. *Bene*. Sometimes the simplest explanations elude us. We come up with more and more fanciful suggestions, then finally, after an hour-long question-and-answer session, pages of drawings and mental gymnastics, with steam coming out of our ears, it dawns on us that Michelangelo is after something perfectly straightforward.

To our huge disappointment there are still no rushes from the first day's shoot – it seems the negatives haven't even been sent off yet. And there I was emphasizing in all the production meetings how important it was that we saw the rushes as early as possible. Now we won't know what we're up against until Tuesday, because the rushes won't go to the lab to be processed till Monday – along with those filmed today and tomorrow. I'm pissed off. Having the rushes would make communication with Michelangelo so much easier. Not even to have had them sent off to the lab was a stupid and trivial economy that might in the end cost us dearly.

As I look back on the day, I remember moments when Michelangelo had tears in his eyes. It moves him when a shot comes out as he'd hoped, or when, after some misunderstanding, we finally get what he wants. Even during the preparations, the moisture in his eyes was often the best indication that we were on the right track. To see this proud and 'aristocratic' man, who never showed signs of weakness in his life, now so sensitive and sometimes so crushed, is something that ought to make us all think about our own 'toughness'.

Saturday 5.11.94 Third day of shoot

At last the weather is slightly better; it's still cloudy, but at least it's not raining buckets. The scene we broke off yesterday seems right today, even though John has gone back to walking in from the right of shot, instead of the left. Michelangelo did the first couple of takes from the left, which was 'more correct', but then his aesthetic sense reasserted itself once more against our logic of 'proper continuity'. Perhaps it's not really a mistake – after all, he's always made his films that way, with some success . . .

We carry on shooting outside, under a cloudy sky but with the rain holding off, a beautiful 'Antonionesque' scene in front of the boutique. But then we have to break for lunch, and I'm furious about this needless waste of what little light there is. It's pointless stopping now, as we're not going to be able to continue beyond three or four o'clock anyway. The reverse shot of the boutique still needs to be filmed, with the window and the water beyond. I hope we manage that. And I hope we can convince Michelangelo to shoot an additional close-up of Sophie, and a matching one of John. He'll need them if he's to bring in the voice-over of the 'director' as presented in the screenplay.

Later. We filmed John's departure, with an interesting 'variation', improvised by Michelangelo: Sophie follows him across to the window, and raises her right hand, as if in farewell.

We just managed a close-up of John, and then the light was gone. We still need to get the corresponding one of Sophie. The light's not a factor, because the window won't be in shot. But these close-ups of faces aren't really Michelangelo's thing. He wasn't very convinced he needed them at all, and during the close-up of John he actually dozed off.

Later still: it's all done, so we've completed the first half-week's shooting schedule on time, and wrapped up our first location, the boutique. Everyone's happy. Including Michelangelo? No one really knows what goes through his mind. After the second close-up, he turned to me and made one of his gestures: *cosi-cosa*. Less than enthusiastic, anyway. I wonder whether he'll even use the close shots in the edit. We'll see . . . That way of building a scene just isn't his style. But Enrica says, and Aruna and I agree with her, that the two close-ups will give him more room for manoeuvre during the editing.

I'm trying to recall how similar scenes were put together in Michelangelo's earlier films. He has a highly individual and rather unorthodox way of approaching the actors with the camera, or of investigating a setting. I often think we're just burdening him with all our suggestions and ideas, instead of enabling him to do it his way. But what is his way? The first shots in the boutique were all certainly 'his'; it would never have occurred to me to do it that way, not least because I would never have considered the zoom as an important tool. So how can we best help him to find his own 'take' on the film? There is a risk that our interpretations of his often rather cryptic utterances don't bring him any nearer, but take him further away from what he wants.

In the evening, Enrica's organized a great 'First Clapboard Party' in a disco in Santa Margarita. We end up bopping till we drop. It's probably not a bad thing for the crew, because they get to know each other a bit. Few of them have worked together before – with the exception of the lighting and the camera crew. The actors in the next episode, Kim Rossi-Stuart and Ines Sastre, are there too.

Amid the flashing lights and the droning techno-beat, I catch an occasional glimpse of Michelangelo's face. He's sitting at the edge of the dance floor, watching all the goings-on, looking rather contented.

Old posters of Michelangelo's films are hung right around the room, brought along by a film club in Milan. I am kindly asked if I'd like to keep one for myself. I choose the poster of *Blow-Up*.

SUNDAY 6.11 94   First rest day

Everyone's recovering from the party and the wild dancing. I have a long meeting with Pierre-Henri Deleau and Felice Laudadio about the plans for a big European film festival in Strasbourg, and a restructuring of the European Film Awards. What about replacing the 'Felix' with a statue called a 'Europa d'Or'?

Vincent Perez is here to try out his costumes and talk about the script. Everything is running about an hour late, because the rain over the last couple of days caused a huge tree to fall across the road leading to the hotel, which meant that Esther Walz, the wardrobe designer, was unable to get through with her sacks of clothes. For hours now we've heard the roaring of chainsaws cutting up the tree.

I have a few words on the telephone with Irene Jacob, who's still in Berlin, where she's filming Mark Peploe's *Victory* with Willem Dafoe as her co-star. She sounds very excited at the prospect of working with Michelangelo. There's sunshine in Berlin, in Rome and in Paris; only up here in the north of Italy was there torrential rain for the past weeks.

Enrica's prediction is that it will be over tomorrow.

Monday 7.11.94   Fourth day of shoot

It has stopped raining. The sky is cloudy, but the clouds are scattered. Michelangelo directs the scene on the harbourside café terrace with great confidence. I think we succeed in following his intuitions, and set up the camera exactly the way he wants it. He's acutely responsive to the location and the feel of the light. It matters to him to have Sophie standing under a tree when she talks to the 'director', to be able to see the sea right at the start, to get a view into the Excelsior Bar...

I try hard not to imagine any shots, much less any sequence of cuts, to remain as open as I can to his language.

Today the nuisance of not having had any rushes to look at is brought home to me. I still don't know what the zoom looks like, and of course that thing gets brought out again today. I can really only guess at what language this film is finding for itself.

Antonioni communicates his intentions to his leads

John and Sophie are really up for everything, and have the patience of saints. On the previous shooting day Sophie stood around in the boutique for hours as her own lighting-double, and John is always on call as well. When he's not in a shot he stays close to the camera for Sophie to focus on, or for off-screen replies. Both of them are willing to do the walks and turns and timings as many times as we ask for, and come up with alternative ways until Michelangelo finally nods. 'Basta.'

I hope the English script is OK. It's a peculiar mixture of all sorts of different people's translations, and it's impossible to assign final responsibility for it, not least as we've just rewritten a few sentences with John and Sophie's help.

In the evening, after we've wrapped, there's a bit of drama. All of a sudden Michelangelo, Enrica, and all three of the producers present – Philippe Carcassonne, Stephane Tchalgadjieff and Felice Laudadio – are sitting up in our room, and the fur is flying. Enrica's in tears, Michelangelo is crossly banging his left hand on the arm of his chair and shouting 'Hoh!', and the producers have run for cover. It's to do with the choice of Claudio di Mauro as Michelangelo's editor. The producers would prefer to have an older, more experienced man for the job. Under pressure, Enrica becomes a veritable tigress, defending Michelangelo's position to the hilt, and rejecting the producers' criticism of Claudio. I tried to conciliate, saying it was widely known that Michelangelo pretty much did his own editing, and therefore all he needed was an able assistant. Actually, I'm not entirely convinced by my own argument; even for a director who edits himself, an experienced editor with a good eye and independent judgement is essential. The debate goes nowhere. None of us knows Claudio. Michelangelo seems to trust him, though, having once made a documentary with him. It's ridiculous to saddle him with an editor he doesn't want. The producers finally realize that. The whole argument only started because they had the best intentions for the film.

That night, we finally get to see the first three days' rushes, and a huge weight is lifted from our minds. Both actors have a wonderfully vivid presence. And while the light isn't great – it hardly could be, given the compromises Alfio has to make for the sake of the second camera – it's unobtrusive and decent. The use of the zoom, as far as I'm concerned, *is* rather obtrusive, and the distortions in the wide-angle range make me wince, but the zooming movements themselves aren't as glaring as I'd feared. Michelangelo's direction is exciting. The pace is deliberate, but it isn't boring. These rushes have the 'modern' look of all his films, and if everything looks as good as this we'll have a beautiful film on our hands. Undeniably, every inch of this footage has Michelangelo's signature on it. No one else would have shot in quite this way.

I feel relieved, too, at the way my suggestions, like the two extra close-ups, seem to fit in. In fact, during the close shots in the boutique, Michelangelo is visibly moved. At the end of the screening, there are once more tears in his eyes. 'Tutto bene.'

The most happy and relieved of all are Alfio and Pino (Giuseppe Venditi, assistant cameraman). Before the rushes they had been under the greatest pressure. For four days, they've shot, and set and focused the light, without any direct feedback or confirmation that they were on the right track. The video monitors are really irrelevant here: they have nothing to say on camera movements, lighting, colour or contrast. Even with a director who can talk, a cameraman won't really be sure until he's seen some rushes. I can only guess what pressure they must have felt – with no rushes and Michelangelo's silence.

Last night Foreman knocked out Cooper in the tenth round. Undisputed world heavyweight champion at the age of forty-five! Incredible. Twenty years ago he had that legendary fight with Muhammad Ali, and now he's a champion once more. Michelangelo is our George Foreman, and he takes a turn on the dance floor with Donata late at night in the hotel bar. The waltz is played by the hotel pianist, whose wife sits on the sofa opposite night after night, gazing adoringly at her husband as he plays. Tonino is very excited, and wants to write a love story based on them right away.

Tuesday 8.11.94   Fifth day of shoot

There's a fly in the ointment today; everything takes too long. Starting first thing. We're filming a long tracking shot for the scene with Sophie and John in which she confesses to him that she killed her father. Once the tracks have been laid, Michelangelo calls for a second camera to film alongside them, on Steadycam. It soon becomes evident that, to make sure it stays out of shot, the Steadycam would have to be so far away from the actors that you would end up with almost the same framing as the camera on tracks. But Michelangelo won't be swayed. And so we shoot with both cameras, though the Steadycam doesn't give us any usable footage. Finally, once we've done the tracking shot, we're able to persuade him to do one take with just the Steadycam, so we at least have one calm, steady walk in front of the actors.

Michelangelo had laid down the rails at a slight angle, which seemed peculiar to me at first, not least because it almost pushed the actors into the water. But then it became clear to me why it wasn't such a bad idea. It means that the beginning of the tracks is always out of shot, whereas on the parallel track I would have proposed, it might have snuck in at the back of the shot. 'I've learned something else today. . .' I say to myself, the lesson being not so much that little mechanical trick as the realization that I should have more trust in Michelangelo. A lot of what at first strikes me as odd, and what I would approach differently, with my different sense of image and philosophy of filming, subsequently turns out to have a reason. And it works too. Just in a different way.

I'm very impressed by John. He always understands right away when he needs to do something to help the camera. Yesterday he once blocked the camera's view of Sophie, and had to walk quite a subtle 'loop' in the next take. It just took him one look in the monitor to see the line he should walk the next time, and he did it perfectly.

By lunchtime, Michelangelo is often flagging. We're gradually getting accustomed to his rhythm, and know that after a short nap during the break he'll be refreshed. He doesn't go away and lie down, he just goes to sleep in his chair.

After lunch today, he panicked when he was confronted with his contract to sign and initial. He finds writing difficult, and his signature is like a child's. His stroke has impaired not just the speech centres of his brain, but also his ability to spell and to form letters. In the end, after struggling through umpteen initiallings and managing a M I C H E L A N G E L O, he fell asleep over the A N T O N I O . . . and when he woke up he was so angry that no amount of persuasion or prospect of money would induce him to add the two remaining letters. The funny thing about it was the despair and the gritted teeth of the producers, Philippe and Stephane, who still weren't in possession of the signed contract they desperately needed to conclude the financing of the film. Afterwards, they came up with a scheme to try and get the two missing letters from him in the course of the evening.

In the afternoon, we're filming on a pier in the harbour. The last bit of Sophie's speech is still to do, where she talks about how generally it's guilt that draws a criminal back to the scene of the crime, but how in her case it was the opposite. Michelangelo stalks about the location for a long time, looking around as though trying to get his bearings. We're all puzzled as to what he wants. Then he comes up with a complicated shot that ends up taking longer to explain than it does to shoot. Twenty people are standing around the wretched monitor, all talking to Michelangelo at once, and all trying to project their own vision of the scene on to him. 'Track', 'Steadycam', 'Fixed camera', 'Pan', 'Sophie walks out of shot', 'John comes into shot'. . . Suggestions are hurled at Michelangelo from all sides. If I were ever caught in a crossfire like that, I know it would drive me crazy. That monitor is a real albatross round our necks, though of course it's indispensable for Michelangelo. Gradually, then, the knot of communication is unpicked, and – thanks especially to the patience of John and Sophie – a lovely scene emerges, which for me is the highlight of all we've done to date. Sophie walks

Antonioni's opinion is solicited concerning the finer points of the source-text

and skips away from the camera in a long arc, then comes back towards it and talks to John, who's still off camera, and only comes in shot when Sophie leaves. In that one masterly shot Michelangelo has captured the place, and Sophie's character and history. Even though it's a relatively long shot, it's always tense and never drags. In the end, Michelangelo has said what he had to say with great intensity and economy. When I imagine a rough-cut of what we've done so far, I'm struck by how laconic and yet lavish he's made it. Place and time, location and character, open themselves up to him, with a minimum of cuts and changes of angle. He only shot what he really had to shoot, apart from the occasionally superfluous use of the second camera. Now he just needs to top and tail his shots, and join them up. Well, maybe a bit more than that.

WEDNESDAY 9.11.94   Sixth day of shoot

Another sticky day. Starting with my accidentally setting the alarm for the wrong time, and waking up an hour late. So I think: swig down a cup of tea, and charge out to the car. But then I run into Andrea in the lobby. There was no rush, because Michelangelo had decided not to shoot the final scene with John down in the little piazza in town, but up here on the hill, around an old tower not far from the hotel. He had stumbled upon this new location in the course of his early morning walk.

There's glorious sunshine, for the first time since we've been here. A shame not to be making the most of it. But Andrea assures me that Michelangelo is convinced the scene would work better up here. By now the heads of production have turned up, and they look pretty agitated. Everyone looks questioningly in my direction. But what am I supposed to say? I'm not the producer, and I'm not the director either; I'm Michelangelo's back-up man, I'm here to help him make *his* film. God knows, I've had plenty of last-minute changes in my own films. We have to follow Michelangelo's instincts, is all I can say. But I feel rather unconvinced by my argument. We're wasting precious time and glorious light. We decide not to bring the crew up here this morning, because that would involve a further loss of time, loading all the equipment on to the trucks and sending them up the difficult road up the hill – we're not even sure the road is passable again. Instead, we're going to go on with the scene that was to follow that first scene in town. After that, in the afternoon, we can come here and film the ending.

So down in the port we finally shoot a scene that is no more than half a sentence in the script, and which we therefore rather underestimated: 'The director nods, and the woman turns on her heel and walks off.' Once again, it takes a while for Michelangelo to get across his concept for the scene, and the fact that he's weighing up two different possible locations for it, but finally we understand what he means. Tracks are laid, and the scene is rehearsed. Then the tracks need to be relaid, because we've misunderstood Michelangelo. The line he showed us was where the actors were supposed to go, not the camera. We make mistakes like that all the time, and Michelangelo only puts us right after he's seen the results on the monitor. There is further room for misunderstanding over the pronouns *lei* and *lui* ('she' and 'he'). It's often difficult for us to guess whether Michelangelo means Sophie or John when he gives us instructions regarding the actors.

Without the video monitor, on which Michelangelo can verify every camera position and movement, we wouldn't stand a chance. But even with his finger on the monitor, he sometimes indicates the opposite of what he wants. He points left, so the camera pans further left, but he wanted it the other way: we were to lose the left part of the shot. He points up, which probably means that the camera should pan upwards, or have a lower angle, but when we do that, he shakes his head: on the contrary, he didn't want to see the top part of the shot any more. Or Michelangelo pinches finger and thumb together, which usually means close the zoom, but it can also mean the opposite. Even his word for it, *chiudi*, can mean both things: open and shut.

So everything rather drags on, particularly as, following the morning's change of plan, we have to wait a couple of hours for Sophie, who wasn't due to be in make-up until later. But then the scene itself turns out really well. Sometimes the number of problems and misunderstandings is in inverse proportion to the end result: the more we struggle with Michelangelo's inability to speak, and the greater the obstacles we have to overcome, the better the scenes turn out. This time, the first shot is done with just one camera; it would have been hard to fit a second one in anyway. Pino, the cameraman, has to pan 240 degrees, and almost ends up in the bay. He gets away with just wet feet and a soaking trouser leg.

It's gradually clouding over now, and our hopes of going up the hill in the afternoon to shoot the final scene recede rapidly.

They recede even further as it becomes evident that the second shot is taking an eternity to set up. The location is a steep flight of stairs leading up from the harbour. Finally, we are able to accommodate the bit of dialogue that Sophie so badly wanted to have in: 'You remind me of . . . somebody.' 'Who?' 'I don't know yet'. . . and it's at this juncture, on the steps immediately before the love scene, that it makes the most sense, too. That little exchange is important for her part, and I can quite see why Sophie wanted it, and was disappointed when she discovered it had been cut. The reason it takes so long is because Alfio suggests a crane shot, which was really a nice idea. But then, while I'm gone for a couple of minutes, the crane is put up a few yards higher, with the result that the cameraman is looking much too steeply down on the actors. And exactly what I was afraid of is happening now: We're looking down on the top of John's head, and his bald patch gleams in the dark alleyway. Michelangelo seems to have a particular aversion to it. It bothered him before, but it's much worse today, following yesterday's rushes. So now, purely on account of John's wretched scalp, Michelangelo decides he'd rather have the scene set up as a big master. And that, of course, doesn't help the actors' lines at all. At the last moment we manage to talk Michelangelo into using a second camera – ironically, it was my suggestion – which would stay semi-close up for the dialogue, and then zoom backwards as the two characters walk up the steps. And that is precisely what Michelangelo's initial idea had been for the steps scene: he laid his hand on mine and gradually opened them out, and later on he did a drawing that showed the scene beginning close up and then widening out.

By the time we've finished that difficult scene it's already half past two, and time for lunch. The minute lunch is over, it starts raining again. Beatrice and I make an attempt to get the camera set up for the next scene – Michelangelo needs another shot of John and Sophie walking, and this time we know the camera position – but by the time the camera has finally been set up in the new location after more endless discussion, it's so dark that we can't film any more. I'm pretty hacked off. Deciding anything is such a palaver; there are always a thousand people having their say, three producers on set and several department heads, plus Enrica and Andrea and me . . . it all takes for ever. Far too often, Michelangelo gets bombarded by all these people, and their ideas and their questions, so he gets to the point where he will just say yes to anything. Which is how it happens that tracks need re-laying, or the crane is hoisted too far.

In the meantime, though, the documentary is going great guns, and Enrica even finds time to conduct short interviews with the actors, Tonino and me. I'm able to fix up a meeting between her and Wilfried Reichart from the film department of the WDR TV station, who might be interested in backing her documentary. A few less money worries would be good for Enrica, considering everything she has on her plate, which she tackles with such boundless energy.

In the evening John asks us to eat with him, but we'd already promised to eat with Michelangelo, who was in a wonderful mood, clowning around and laughing, and for the first time expressly asked Donata and me to dinner. We'd never seen him that cheerful before. At dinner, though, Michelangelo makes a very different impression, and when we ask him what the matter is, he crosses himself several times and says 'Morto', to indicate his approaching end. He's been doing that for a long time, Enrica reassures us, and the effect of his saying it was anything but morbid – on the contrary, it was cathartic and kept him going.

Then he eats a big bowl of whipped cream for pudding, and suddenly he's on top form again, dancing in the hotel bar with Enrica, Agnes and Donata.

Meanwhile, I'm sitting at my desk, feeling pretty shattered. I'm learning that it's much more tiring being a spectator than a director. Not getting involved seems to cost me more energy than getting involved. Getting the crew going is really exhausting, and I can appreciate what a difficult job the assistant directors have. It's a job I've never done, so the situation is completely new to me. Maybe I should stay in the background even more? At the same time, though, I can't help feeling a strong connection with Michelangelo, with the script and the actors and the locations. I really identify with this project – after all, I was involved from the start. So every wasted half-hour and all the waiting around hurts me. The worst thing is witnessing how Michelangelo's moments of energy and concentration are often allowed to go to waste, because the crew's rhythm is out of sync with his, so he's sitting there alert and impatient but unable to do anything, and by the time they're ready to shoot, he's exhausted and wiped out. We must learn to adjust to his rhythms better.

I catch the weather on TV, and feel annoyed with myself for not insisting on shooting the final scene this morning after all. According to the forecast, those hours of sunshine will be the last for some time. The rain is once more lashing down outside, and the wind is howling round the hotel.

But our worries are pretty minor really. The flooding in northern Italy has cost 100 lives already, and left thousands of people homeless. Our designer, Thierry Flamand, who's gone on ahead to prepare the next episode, reports that our next week's locations are under threat: in Ferrara they're afraid that the main bridge over the Po may be washed away.

THURSDAY 10.11.94   Seventh day of shoot

Today, it's the love scene between Sophie and John that's on the agenda. We're filming inside the old turreted building at whose doors we began the film a week ago. Yet again it's teeming down, and there's a howling gale. And yet again it takes us an age to get going. Once a crew has fallen into this kind of sluggish tempo it's difficult, sometimes impossible, to speed them up.

Yesterday Michelangelo indicated to me that he wants to be alone with the actors today. I think he's right. The scene and the room are both so intimate that it'll be hard enough to find a corner for Michelangelo, with his two monitors and the two cameras. Nobody knows how he intends to shoot it. We gather that he intends his principal camera to be the Steadycam, which will move around the actors all the time. Three shots are planned . . .

. . . Or so we thought, but what he means, it turns out, is three cameras. And then he's royally pissed off that we only have two – he simply can't accept it, he's furious, and keeps banging his hand against the arm of his chair. He got it into his head that he has to have three cameras, even though there's no

'Naked as the day they were born': Malkovich and Marceau throw themselves into their love scene

way on earth you could possibly fit three cameras into that tiny space, never mind that one of them is going to be cruising round the bed on a dolly.

It might be even trickier than we'd supposed . . .

And it is, but then again, it isn't. I'd actually planned on having a quiet day, because Michelangelo had indicated that he wanted me to stay outside along with everyone else. But then at the last moment he summons me into the room, and I end up being in the thick of it. Alfio and I manage to talk Michelangelo into filming with one camera first, and the other later. The dolly and the Steadycam would just get in each other's way; we see that from the very first run-through. The camera on the dolly registers the shadow of the Steadycam, and the Steadycam has the rails in shot. Nightmare. So for once Michelangelo doesn't film with two cameras in tandem, but arranges two shots in succession, which also gives Alfio the chance to set a better light. Then, at Michelangelo's insistence, the Steadycam is replaced by

Sophie Marceau in half-profile: an image that would later grace the film's poster

a second dolly, on the far side of the bed. That'll make it easier to edit too.

Initially, Sophie is very worried about the total nudity that Michelangelo demands from both actors, with an unequivocal gesture and a further word in his repertoire: 'Nuda.' 'How much of me can you see?' she asks, but then, when no one answers, and I too only shrug, she realizes it's rather a hopeless question, and that she's probably in shot from head to foot. For a moment I see her struggling with herself. John is hesitating too. The two of them exchange glances, and then, in unspoken agreement, submit to the inevitable.

They hold a whispered consultation. The ensuing scene will always be an example for me of the great courage and mutual trust of two actors, not to mention their skill. They appear wholly uninhibited, playing the scene naked as the day they were born, exchanging passionate kisses and rolling around the bed in one another's arms.

It's not my thing at all, more so as I'm sitting so close to the bed I could reach out and touch both of them. I prefer to look away, instead keeping one eye on the indistinct images on the monitor and the other eye on Michelangelo, to observe his reactions and convey them to the actors for the next take.

The scene is shot several times, and then from the other side too. The two dolly-shots end up taking so long that the light is waning outside. Alfio sensibly suggests that we buck the running order, and go on to the shot where the window appears. That comes off surprisingly easily, and leaves us with only one shot left, which we coax Michelangelo into doing: a transition between John getting out of bed and the farewell at the window. Sophie sits up in bed, and we see her in half-profile from behind. That turns out particularly well, and things improve. I had found, for instance, that the second camera position was distinctly unflattering. At Michelangelo's insistence it remained very open, showing the two actors from head to foot in their birthday suits, but from a low angle, so it was mostly their buttocks and armpits.

But even that angle gave us a few good moments, and ultimately Michelangelo will assemble the scene on the cutting table anyway. The two actors have generously given him their all.

We all feel we've made a lot of progress. The rest of this episode is pretty straightforward – at least compared to what we've managed over the last few days.

In the evening there's a Mass in the church for Enrica's mother. Afterwards we go on to a ceremony at which Michelangelo is being honoured – the Commune of Portofino is giving him a medallion for his work. I am presented with a large bottle of olive oil, which makes me very happy.

Late at night we watch the rushes, which Enzo, the projectionist, has brought himself by car from Rome. It all looks very good, and Donata and I are especially impressed by Sophie. It's in the rushes that you get the clearest sense of the work of the actors, and Sophie is really convincing. While very sparing with gestures and facial expressions, she's managed to give the rather vague character of the parricide some dignity and plausibility. I must confess I was surprised by how good she was. That's what comes of sitting behind the monitor the whole time: you only see a fraction of what the actors are really doing. But there's really no alternative: it's only from the monitors that I can get a sense of what pleases Michelangelo and what doesn't. And that's really the sum total of my job. I decide not to use a monitor at all when I move on to my own shoot, and just watch the actors. I hope I can still do that. There is something habit-forming about having those things on set.

One more day, and we'll have finished the first episode. Once again, I'm shattered, more exhausted than I would be if I'd been directing.

Friday 11.11.94 Eighth day of shoot

At seven a.m. we spend an hour doing a belated recce to see where Michelangelo wants to film the final sequence in the afternoon. A tower up above the hotel has been mooted, and a path on the hillside with a view over the bay of Portofino and the Mediterranean. Today Michelangelo doesn't appear to like the tower especially; I have the feeling he's just going through the motions, and that his thoughts have already moved on to somewhere else. But where? The production crew, concerned to get the last day's shooting done on time, is keen to make him commit to a location. But all their pressure just seems to annoy Michelangelo. The production crew has every reason to be concerned: we only have permission to film in a particular area, we're not allowed inside the tower, the most we can do is show John walking up the steps to it, etc. etc.

When we get back to the hotel after an hour of wandering about, I keep seeing Michelangelo looking down at the swimming pool, and on one occasion pointing at it. No one takes him up on it. I don't ask him about it, because he's already heard the question 100 times this morning: 'Is that the location you want?'

Malkovich in pensive mood above the bay of Portofino

In the morning we work on a couple of pick-up shots from the first, rained-off day: John follows Sophie down the narrow path into the town. And in the afternoon we find ourselves not shooting in any of the places we looked at in the morning, but at the swimming pool next to the hotel. Once again, there's that tense spectacle – as with the scene on the pier – of Michelangelo walking up and down, feeling the place, testing it out with his eyes, and finally letting the camera make a single, very simple movement, namely a reverse zoom that takes in the entire scene. He begins, this time, with a close-up of John sitting on a deckchair, brooding (held for a long time, so it could be used for the narrator's voice-over); then it gradually opens out until you see the bay in the background and the pool in the foreground. Finally, John gets up and walks out of shot. That does it for this episode, really. But Michelangelo does another take that begins with the extended zoom on the boats in the bay, and then pulls back to a wide shot in which John comes into the picture, then stops and looks up – not out to sea, because then we'd have his bald patch, but back up the hill. The second camera, placed higher up, does the opposite movement: it begins tight on John, and goes out to show a wide shot of the bay under the evening sky. The two shots would seem to be mutually exclusive. But the light is lovely, and everything goes very smoothly, even though, as always, there's a lot of tension until we've worked out what it is that Michelangelo wants. Then it's too dark to carry on, and we've finished. The first episode has been completed on time. Everyone's happy, the producers are ecstatic, and we go around snapping group pictures in the dying light until we've used up all our film.

Enrica, Andrea and I go up to a hotel room, to make a first, provisional recording of John's voice narrating, to give Michelangelo something to go on when he's in the cutting room. John gives his lines an utterly individual melody. Very few actors have such a distinctive voice that they can really make a text their own. I can think of Bruno Ganz, Peter Falk, Gene Hackman and Jeanne Moreau. By the time Jean-Pierre Ruh has switched off his Nagra, the first episode really is finished.

The rushes of the love scene are much better than I'd dared hope, and not nearly as risqué as I'd feared. The second camera does indeed show mainly bottoms and hairy armpits, but there are a couple of good moments in the footage as well. Alfio's 'morning light' is simple but effective, and shows a grey-blue, twilit room, lit only from the window. Their farewells are moving, especially the close-up of Sophie in half-profile – in which, I'm pleased to say, I had a hand.

Sophie is clearly shocked by her torrid sex scene with John, but she seems calm enough. She'd never done anything like this before, she confesses later, much less nude. John is impressed with how gamely she went along with everything, although – as he was in a better position than anyone to appreciate – she was seething inside. Sophie's part ended up being much harder to play than John's, who played more of an observer figure. She was the dynamic one. It's actually the opposite of how it appeared on paper, in the script. Only during the actual filming did Michelangelo develop the scenes from the woman's point of view. The fact that the man appears as 'the director', and observes the woman with fascination, now seems all the more logical. All the camera movements were with reference to the woman. The static element was always the man. The construction of the scenes we shot this week seems like a microcosm of all Michelangelo's films. When Sophie walks into shot on the pier, and then walks round in a great loop and back towards the camera, there's an echo of *L'Avventura* there: behind Sophie you can identify the shadow of Monica Vitti.

SATURDAY 12.11.94   Rest and travel day

As always on rest days during a shoot, I wake up at seven and can't get back to sleep. It's lovely and sunny outside. It's the first time Portofino has chosen to show us its best side. But actually it's a good thing for the film that we didn't have more sunshine. The story would have suffered, and become a tawdry little romance. The rain and the murky light have helped Michelangelo and Alfio.

For the first time we get the chance to swim in the lovely pool where we filmed yesterday. The sea water is icy, but there's a warm layer of rain water on top of it.

Last night we had a meal with John and Sophie during which we laughed a lot, especially at John's stories. He's flying back to Lisbon today, to carry on with the filming of Manoel de Oliveira's *Il Convento*, with Catherine Deneuve as his co-star. Sophie is driving back to Paris. We assure her she's made a wonderful job of it. Michelangelo hadn't been able to tell her anything, beyond how to come in shot, when to turn, where to walk. When he wanted her more agitated, he asked her for agitation, without being able to give her any motivation. All the other feelings, every bit of psychology and the whole orientation of her character, were things Sophie had to find for herself. That gave her a freedom that I'm sure will appear in the film. Remembering Michelangelo's early films, that freedom seems like an aura that all his women characters seemed to have about them. They never had to fulfil any particular expectation, they weren't formed in advance, but they manifested their mysterious being with every movement and every turn of the head. In her movements and gestures and twists and turns, the actress plays herself; she is strikingly unprotected and vulnerable, which makes her all the more 'touching'. No wonder that *gira* ('turn around' or 'turn away') remained one of the few directing words in Michelangelo's depleted vocabulary. The direction, however – whether with the head or the body or the eyes – often took a lot of trial and error to establish, before the actors and the rest of us hit upon whatever Michelangelo meant by any particular instance of *gira*. He likes the turn of the head, and in some shots, Sophie evoked memories of Jeanne Moreau in *La Notte*. At any rate, in Michelangelo's eyes, Sophie has added herself firmly to the list of 'Antonioni heroines'. More than anything, one little gesture of hers will stay with me, something she did almost clandestinely, before every take: hurriedly making the sign of the cross and tensing her fists and forearms, like a football player about to take a penalty.

Donata and I drive on our own to Ferrara, by way of Padua and Bologna. 'Ferrara!' is one of Michelangelo's few words. Why can he say that particular name and not another? He can also say 'Enrica' – to Enrica of course, but also to other members of the crew. It's his one proper name, and it has to do for others as well. It's hard to understand how the brain does that: be capable of understanding language, but unable to produce it, either written or spoken. As Michelangelo isn't capable of spelling, he can't use a typewriter either. That makes it all the more remarkable that a man who has difficulty speaking, is unable to write, impaired in his mobility, and unable to walk unaided, can yet exert a grip on this film, can direct it with skill and authority, and thereby project his inner vision into the outside world.

He's even quite sophisticated about how he does it; *malin*, as they say in France. Nobody understood, for example, why he insisted on setting aside three shooting days for the dialogue scene between the 'director' and the woman. It was only when we were actually filming in Portofino that it became clear that these three days in the schedule enabled him to film whatever wasn't in the script, and what he therefore had no way of predicting beforehand. The scenes that impressed me most, and where he showed his full mastery (the final scene with John, and the scenes with the two of them on the quayside and on the steps) didn't come from the script at all, but were created out of the place and the drama, and in such a way that no one but Michelangelo would have come up with them. I want to ensure that he gets this same kind of space in the remaining episodes as well, so that he can film things he is unable to explain to us in advance.

In fact, from what I know of Michelangelo's early films, his way of working hasn't actually changed that much at all. In his early films, his crew and his actors often didn't know what he had in mind. 'No so!' ('I don't know') isn't just his standby now, in his aphasia; he also used to say that on earlier films when he was expected to discuss what he would only know on the day.

Working without a script is something I've often done myself, and many times I've driven my crews and my actors to distraction, as a result of not knowing what I would do next. But my way of 'not knowing yet' is probably not the same as Michelangelo's, just as the solutions we come up with aren't the same. Both of us, I think, like to be open to our locations. But while I tend to see and to think out of the subjectivity of my characters, Michelangelo sees and thinks in a cooler, more distant way; still bound up, of course, with the people and the place, but not from within them, more looking down on them, not in a condescending way, but as a storyteller might manipulate his characters, from above.

I suppose 'separation' is his theme: parting, incompatibility, alienation. I've had similar labels attached to my films; the American critics have always seen me in terms of their three 'A's: 'Angst, Alienation and America'. But for me, the films are far more to do with 'wanting-to-be-at-one', and the alienation in them is generally overcome during and by the film, whereas in Michelangelo's films it persists, though minutely analysed.

Antonioni at twilight

Maybe I'll return to the subject some other evening – I'm too tired to go on now. We're staying at a hotel in Ferrara that used to be a private dwelling in the fifteenth century. All the rooms are 'plushissimo', with flowered wallpaper, four-poster beds and pink sofas. I'm glad we're filming in winter. I can just imagine how hopeless it would be trying to catch mosquitoes in terrain like that!

Sunday 13.11.94   Rest day

Or not exactly, as Michelangelo wants us to drive out to Comacchio at ten o'clock, to have another look at our locations. The last I'd heard, last night, it was going to happen in the afternoon. So when Andrea calls us at half past nine to 'remind us that we're leaving at ten', we haven't had breakfast and are pretty cheesed off to be the last to know, and to have to chase after the others. I don't know what's been said to Michelangelo, but he seems pretty pissed off that we're late, and he seems annoyed too that Donata and I didn't eat with him yesterday – but if that's what he wanted, he should have said so. His rather cold and offhand attitude gets to us both, especially Donata. But when we take it up with him in the evening, everything seems hunky-dory again, and he laughs at all our jokes. Because he can't speak, we're probably always too quick to read things into everything he does say, and take every 'Via!' or 'Fuori' or 'Niente' rather too personally.

The locations in Comacchio are fantastic, especially the street with the long, long arcade. Thierry Flamand has done sterling work. With his crew of painters and set-dressers, he's converted an office building into a hotel, and so convincingly you'd swear it had never been anything else. (Admittedly, they're still hammering, sawing and painting away.) In the midst of this foggy and melancholy landscape, this 'building site' has an unexpectedly joyful atmosphere. There are children jumping around, a ghetto blaster is playing, and Michelangelo is greeted on all sides with eager expectation. I hope the 'maestro' likes the new set . . .

Michelangelo takes a good look at everything, seems favourably impressed, and in the end changes just a couple of little details: the neon HOTEL sign is put over the balcony, and in the front lobby the frosted glass pane is replaced with clear glass.

In the late afternoon, there are costume and make-up trials for Ines Sastre and Kim Rossi-Stuart. Then we do a read-through. Ines is Spanish, and her Italian isn't especially good, certainly not up to pages and pages of dialogue. Michelangelo seems to have forgotten that, and doesn't understand why we can't just shoot everything in Italian. Someone suggests that she say her longer speeches in French. They would have to be synched later. But that's not really satisfactory either. I finally suggest working it into the script somewhere that the Carmen character doesn't speak good Italian. She might ask Silvano if he minded whether she spoke French or something. We agree on that. Ines is relieved, because she's learned her part in French, and she would be very uncertain in Italian.

That evening, in Comacchio's little art museum, Michelangelo is awarded a prize for his work. We break up fairly early for the drive back to Ferrara. Donata and I have decided not to stay with the crew in Comacchio, but to go back to Ferrara so as not to leave Michelangelo all alone there. There's thick fog on the motorway on the thirty-mile drive back, and as a result it takes three times as long as it did this morning. I suspect we may get that kind of fog every night.

MONDAY 14.11.94 Ninth day of shoot

And our first with our new pair, Ines Sastre and Kim Rossi-Stuart. We drive from Ferrara to Comacchio in thick fog, and there's fog when we start filming too – just what the screenplay ordered.

In the first shot Carmen comes riding towards us on her bicycle under the arcades. A car drives down the street, passes her, stops and hoots. Silvano climbs out and runs over to her. He asks if she knows of somewhere to stay in the vicinity, and she directs him to a small hotel very close by, where she's staying herself. The lines are said, as written, in Italian. Then Silvano gets back in his car and drives off, all without a cut. First of all Michelangelo shoots a very beautiful tracking shot, under the arcade, looking out across the street. Then, after a few takes, he tries out a fixed camera position and shoots everything from one point of view, again under the arcades. The second camera is in on the act from the start, tight on Carmen, but when we therefore propose a matching close-up of Silvano, Michelangelo rejects the idea out of hand: 'Basta.' He doesn't need a close-up of Silvano, and so he won't shoot it. It would have been over in five minutes, but no, he's not interested. Even when Alfio and I go to him with the argument that he could always make his mind up about the shot later, in the cutting room, Michelangelo remains obdurate. The man doesn't interest him; the close-up is only for the woman. Gradually I understand: the man appears in the film because his eyes see the woman, and for that reason the camera shows her, and not him. *Basta.*

Ines is very beautiful, probably too beautiful for the schoolteacher she's supposed to be playing. You can just about tell that she's relying on her beauty to get her through, and that she has more experience as a model than as an actress. Of course, she's still very much in awe of Michelangelo and the huge crew. I hope she'll relax. The success of the episode rather depends on it. I like Kim, with his quiet, melancholy manner, though it's probably a little too restrained for Michelangelo. He likes his men more resolute and heroic, and gestures to Kim accordingly.

The scene is shot surprisingly quickly, not least because

Antonioni and his new leading male, Kim Rossi-Stuart

Michelangelo doesn't require any further set-ups, except for one with two cameras. So by half past ten we're already up at the hotel. Things are not quite ready for us, and Thierry's crew of decorators are rather taken aback by our early arrival. No one expected us before lunch.

We talk to Michelangelo about the bit of dialogue that will explain why Ines is speaking French. Michelangelo isn't happy with any of the suggestions and has a different idea, which he is unable to explain to us, and which we're unable to guess. Finally he draws two women with a big 'S' next to them. 'Tutte due!' he keeps saying, pointing at Ines. We don't get it. After a lot of guessing, we do. He's referring to Ines and her mother, who's with her on set, and the 'S' is for 'Spanish'. They talk Spanish together, and Michelangelo wants Tonino's script to say that Ines is Spanish, not French. Though in spite of that, she's to talk to Silvano in French. Whew! They're sometimes such simple things, and he needs to find such elaborate ways of getting us to understand them.

We may have been quick this morning, but we're miserably slow in getting the next shot: Silvano arrives at the hotel, walks in, we see him talking to the manager at the front desk, then he comes out again, gets in his car and drives off. Michelangelo seems unhappy about something, but once again we don't know what. By now it's too dark to go on to anything else. It's the end of filming for today.

Tuesday 15.11.94 Tenth day of shoot

The same thick fog, the same long crawl out to Comacchio. Overnight, Michelangelo has devised a new opening shot of the hotel, as I all but predicted yesterday. I'm not quite sure whether the new shot is to replace yesterday's or is in addition to it. It's tricky for the crew, because all the cars and trucks have to be reparked, not once but twice. So, first of all everybody's running around like headless chickens. A big crew like ours takes time to react to new instructions.

The heavy dolly is hauled on to the roof of the gate, because the new beginning includes a tracking shot over the roof. Then, unfortunately, the fog lifts, so the interior has to be re-lit. If we get any more sunshine, the conditions will be so unlike what they were yesterday that we won't be able to shoot at all. But we're spared that, thank God: the sun is obscured, and we're happily fogbound once more. The shot turns out beautifully, and Michelangelo looks far chirpier. *Tutto bene.*

The next scene offers more in the way of difficulties. Michelangelo had supposed we could pitch the camera on the other side of a little stream that flows behind the 'hotel', and that, using two cameras, he could get an establishing shot of the hotel and a tighter one of the window, so that he could capture the meeting of Carmen and Silvano from a distance – out of earshot of their conversation. So we put the two cameras on the other side of the stream, but by this stage we're actually so far away that even with a tele-lens we can hardly see anything of what's going on through the window. Michelangelo had imagined it rather differently. He gets more and more disillusioned with the entire scene, to the point of losing interest in it altogether. I have the impression he's thinking of taking a completely different approach, but he hasn't got there yet, so he's just letting us go ahead and film these shots, to play for time. So we shoot them regardless, and I do my best to make them somehow useful, or at least bits of them, so they could perhaps be cut together later. But each time I look up from the monitor at his face, I see there's not much hope of that.

The mood here in Comacchio is completely different to Portofino. But it's not just the fog that's getting everyone down. We now know what filming with Michelangelo is like, and the eager intensity there was at the start has now given way to a rather torpid daily routine. What people are missing is encouragement and approval. But that's exactly what's not forthcoming from Michelangelo. No thanks, no gesture of appreciation, either for the actors nor for those on the technical side. But if you can believe the reports of his earlier shoots, that's how it was then too.

After lunch Michelangelo is in a black mood. When Esther Walz, the costume designer, comes in with the extra who's going to play the waitress in the restaurant, they are both greeted with a 'Via!' from him: that's what he thinks of the proposed costume. Esther naturally has an alternative ready, and that duly finds favour.

We try to glean from Michelangelo what we're going to do next; whether we're going on to the next scene with Carmen and Silvano, or re-jigging the whole sequence we've just shot. He gets very irritable, probably because he doesn't know what he's going to do himself. Finally he rejects every suggestion, and keeps saying 'Io' while pointing repeatedly at himself, as if to say: '*I'm* deciding this, you keep out of this, this is my film.' We're in despair, especially the producers. If he re-shoots the beginning tomorrow, that will mean we've achieved precisely nothing today, except the extra shot we did this morning, and that was only to replace one we did yesterday. In the end, Alfio succeeds in convincing Michelangelo that the idea of filming the building from outside hasn't worked, and that we need to do the scene inside, and close to his two leads. Michelangelo tests out Alfio's proposal, once everyone else on the crew has been turfed out so that, for once, we have some silence, and . . . he likes it! He rehearses the scene with the actors, and Andrea and I are delighted to find that we don't need any extra dialogue and Tonino's existing text will do fine. Phew! That sorts out all the questions for tomorrow. It's going to take Alfio several hours, anyway, to get all the lights right for the interior, so we wrap.

In the evening we look at the rushes from the final day's filming in Portofino, and the first in Comacchio. There are a few good shots among them, especially the foggy shot of the arcades. I hope Michelangelo will leave that beginning uncut: the first encounter of Carmen and Silvano is outstandingly effective in that single shot. The second camera close-up of Carmen is so poorly framed as to be completely unusable, and Michelangelo and Alfio agree after the screening that it will have to be done again. But does he really need it? I still can't see how he'll integrate the close-up of Carmen with the long shot, without the equivalent countershot of Silvano.

The last rushes from Portofino are the closing shots of John by the pool. I really take exception to the excessive use of the zoom here, when it's not justified by any other camera movement. Michelangelo also seems a bit unhappy about seeing John, rather bizarrely framed, hunkered down on the bottom edge of the picture. With hindsight, I'm annoyed with myself for not being more forceful with my suggestion that we give John a proper chair instead of his deckchair. That would have helped the framing, and John would have been a bit more mobile as well. But Michelangelo turned that idea down flat. Donata reckons I should make my suggestions to him in private. No director would find it easy to listen to another director's suggestions in front of his whole crew, she says. I'd find it just as difficult myself. Generally, I've been putting my ideas to him indirectly, via Enrica or Andrea, for that very reason.

It's once again apparent that the second camera footage is nowhere near the quality of the first. There was a zoom on that too, but if it isn't handled with the utmost sensitivity, it goes wrong. This time there's a socking great out-of-focus bush in the closing shot, so I'm not surprised to hear Michelangelo muttering 'Niente!' in the dark beside me. It was hard to tell in advance that it would be as bad as that, because the monitor is so small. That evening I'd suggested that the camera needed to be a bit over to the right, to miss out that bush, but nothing was done. On the one hand, I need to put my views across more forcefully when I see something that Michelangelo may have missed; on the other hand, I need to be even more tactful about how I get that across.

Driving home to Ferrara through the fog, I feel pretty unhappy with myself. If I'd put my observations and criticisms over more clearly, these rushes would have been the better for it – and more like the way Michelangelo would have wished them to be. And that, as I understand much more clearly than I did even a week ago, is my job. The other day Stephane told me I

Wenders at work on his portions of the scenario

was an angel, and that's true inasmuch as I'm supposed to be invisible. Any suggestions from me should be confined to making improvements within Michelangelo's overall *mise en scène*, rather than introducing any new ideas of my own. I need to learn to be so invisible that I no longer see what *I* would like to see, but keep my vision within his, and put any suggestions and alternatives strictly from within *that*.

It might be termed 'selfless', but in a sense that I've never known before. My task wasn't clear to me in advance, just as the whole course of the shoot with Michelangelo wasn't clear, and no one on the crew could have predicted what their work would be like. Now we all know a bit better. The difficulty is finding out with each new day to what extent we can rely on Michelangelo implicitly, and at what point we must realize that he needs our help, because he doesn't have quite the control over story and images that he would like to have.

I see from the rushes that we have to watch Ines, because she has a tendency to smile too much. It's a 'bad habit' from her time as a model. I like Kim, with his mild, unobtrusive manner. He's stunning-looking as well, and the hordes of teenagers that

Michelangelo and Enrica

wait for him for hours at the gate every day are proof of his popularity in Italy.

Michelangelo and Enrica really have got an amazing cast together. I can remember how obsessively Michelangelo used to pore over magazines and film journals, look at videos and scrutinize photographs. He first spotted Ines in a fashion magazine, and even though other actresses were discussed for her part from time to time, he kept going back to her picture.

WEDNESDAY 16.11.94   Eleventh day of shoot

Today Donata and I head out a little later than usual, as it'll take Alfio a while to sort out the lighting. For once, the fog has lifted, and we get our first look at the landscape between Ferrara and Comacchio. It makes me keen not to confine my own episode to the city, but to go out into the Po Valley. There are some wonderful nooks in Comacchio, lots of canals and bridges, and a most peculiar tower that looks like a gigantic candlestick. I hope we get a chance to scout around a bit for my own shoot, before we have to move on from here.

Then we shoot the scene that didn't work out yesterday, but from inside instead of outside. Alfio suggests two cameras, but Michelangelo only wants one. He wants it to follow Silvano through the door and then pan to Carmen, who's sitting in the next room, showing her looking up and recognizing him. But it doesn't work out the way Michelangelo envisages. Finally, he agrees to the second camera set-up as originally proposed, and both the scene and the beginning of the dialogue go well.

For the continuation, Michelangelo has two cameras set up in the 'restaurant' next door. It's quite a complicated thing to do ina small room, but it works out well enough. He's added something to the script: Silvano trying to kiss Carmen, and her turning away with a smile. It's a nice scene, except that Ines still has a bit of trouble with the words. She's not yet an experienced actress, and so she tends to 'recite' her lines a bit. But after some initial uncertainty she improves a lot, and is even bold enough to ask Michelangelo for one more take. He lets her have one, and it turns out to be her best. It is tough for Ines, having to switch about between Italian, a language she barely knows, and French, which isn't her native language either. Her Spanish accent comes through in both, and because the Spanish tend to speak their language faster and more monotonously than the French do, her French lines sound a bit mechanical. But she is getting more confident all the time, and manages to drop her nervous smile. The scene is wrapped to the general satisfaction of all of us.

Michelangelo always seems more sure of himself when he's had a chance to sleep on a scene. Today's shooting is very confident, after yesterday's false start. The additional shot of Silvano's arrival was better second time round too. The same thing happened in Portofino during those first few days' shooting in the boutique.

At dusk we take a look at the main location for tomorrow's filming: the arcades again. This is where we're going to shoot the long dialogue between Carmen and Silvano which, according to the script, is supposed to begin in daylight and end at night. From our very first script discussions we'd never been entirely sure how that was going to work. Michelangelo had indignantly turned down the suggestion of any leaps in time, as he wants the scene to respect the unities. But how was there going to be daylight at the beginning of it and night at the end? Michelangelo has never been able to give us an answer to that, and as a result Beatrice has always feared for her schedule. There's the potential for a huge snarl-up in that one scene.

As we look at the location, we quickly realize that there's no way we can light the 200-yard-long arcade for a night shoot. There's nowhere to hide the lights, either in the arcade or outside it. There are no buildings opposite, just a large, open sports field. Alfio manages to persuade Michelangelo that we have to shoot in the daytime, possibly into the dusk, but not at night. That's for tomorrow then, and we also want to retake the close-up of Carmen for the opening scene, which didn't look good in the rushes.

47

Michelangelo is in a high good humour over supper, and laughs a lot. With the help of gestures and drawings, he tells us how in *Deserto rosso* they'd painted a whole forest white, only for it all to wash off in overnight rain.

THURSDAY 17.11.94 Twelfth day of shoot

In addition to doing another close-up of Ines, it turns out, to general astonishment – purely on Michelangelo's own orders; no one dared suggest it – that we're doing two over-shoulder shots of the scene, plus a close-up of Kim as well! I'm thinking that while Michelangelo hasn't completely re-evaluated the first day's work, the rushes must have shown him that he can't rely on his female lead in the second episode as he did in the first. However beautiful Ines is, she simply hasn't yet got Sophie's actorly ability. She's only twenty, after all. Kim, on the other hand, has, and when you watch him, all precision and calm, it's easy to imagine that he'll one day be one of the greats. So I can understand why Michelangelo is now belatedly shifting his emphasis – though we won't know that for sure until the editing. I'm more persuaded than ever that Michelangelo can indeed hold an entire sequence of shots in his mind's eye.

Tonino Guerra and Laura his wife visit the set, and as always when Tonino's around, there's a lot of laughing and everything seems quite effortless. He pulls out a whole page of new dialogue for the long scene with Carmen and Silvano – the scene we're shooting under the arcade this afternoon. Andrea and I exchange silent looks of consternation, and then we both set about persuading Tonino to abandon his notion: Ines could never master a new set of lines in a couple of hours, and in Italian at that. Besides, the content isn't all that different from what's in the script, just rephrased. Tonino sees our point and, with a laugh, he puts the sheet of paper back in his pocket.

The sun comes out at the worst possible time for us, and drives away the last of the fog. We decide to embark on the long dialogue scene after lunch. That gives us time to re-lay the

Ines Sastre: captured in the video monitor

tracks. They've been laid – all forty yards of them – right down the middle of the street, which means we'd have to shoot with a wide-angle lens, which would completely distort the beautiful arcade. I said as much to the grips and to Alfio, but because Michelangelo had indicated the middle of the street, the tracks were duly laid down the middle of the street. Giancarlo, the stage manager, re-lays them with the patience of a saint.

Especially where camera positions are concerned, Michelangelo's instructions tend to be pretty vague. It isn't until the camera's been set up, and he can look through it, or see the shot on his monitor, that he gets more precise. And we're often unable to tell from his drawings where the camera should be. When we go out on a new location, we're never quite sure what Michelangelo is pointing to: is it the camera position or the actors? After cross-questioning him several times, we're often no wiser. 'Gira!' he shouts. But is it the camera or the actors that should turn? Not until everything's ready, and the actors are moving about in front of the camera, does it become clear what that 'Gira!' is meant to apply to.

(I remember how long it took us to understand that, in the

love scene between John and Sophie. It wasn't Sophie who was to get up out of bed – which is how it was in the script – but John. Because Michelangelo can't cope with names and often gets 'he' and 'she' muddled up, he kept replying 'Si' to all our questions, so we thought the scene called for her to get up and walk away from the bed. 'Bene.' But when Sophie gets up, Michelangelo gestures in dismay: 'Niente!' It was *John* he meant.)

During the lunch break we look at some rushes, and they make pretty dispiriting viewing. The two shots of the hotel from across the street that we took the day before yesterday are even more of a disappointment than we'd feared. All that charging around really didn't pay off. The long shot is *so* long that you can't see anything of what's happening in the house at all, and the wretched zoom has no resolution at that range. I did my best to get the camera crew at least to demonstrate what a fixed 25 lens would do. I even picked the thing up and handed it to them, but no, Pino and his assistant had to have the zoom, because 'that way the maestro can choose exactly the framing he wants'. True, and that's why (unfortunately) we keep using the damned thing, but lots of unusable footage is no good to the maestro either. The second camera is completely off in its framing, and once again completely unusable. Michelangelo ostentatiously nods off during the screening, and afterwards just sadly shakes his head. His inability to speak is worse for us when he can't use drawings or gestures to express what he's thinking.

In the afternoon we start on the dialogue scene. As planned, we begin with a long tracking shot. That comes off nicely. We carry on under the arcades, using the Steadycam, retreating in front of the actors. Carlo, the Steadycam operator, does it well, but Michelangelo can't see any of it on his monitor. The transistor's range simply isn't long enough, and there's just a blizzard on the screen in front of him. I suggest putting Michelangelo in his wheelchair directly behind the camera. That way he can see and hear the actors, and get a clear, though small, image on his Watchman. To begin with it seems to work, and it's a great

Sastres and Rossi-Stuart by the arcades at dusk

thing to see Michelangelo in the thick of the action like that. He puts pressure on us to shoot quickly, so we end up forgetting about the lighting and just turn over in the rest of the daylight. But by only the second shot, Michelangelo slumps over in his wheelchair. He's barely able to concentrate on the third, and finally he dozes off during the take. We interrupt the shoot. It was too tiring for him. I'm alarmed to see him really helpless for the first time. My idea with the wheelchair now strikes me as a bad one, and I'm sorry I suggested it.

By now it's too dark to shoot the final shot, with the end of the dialogue and the kiss. What now? Another scene he hasn't managed to complete, and now we're basically two full days behind schedule. No chance of getting out of Comacchio on Saturday. Tuesday seems more realistic, maybe even Wednesday. Beatrice has already had a few sleepless nights because of not knowing how to make up the delays, but she's really not at fault. With Michelangelo we're simply unable to shoot any other way – and certainly no quicker. A lot of the crew are full of doubts, and struggling in the teeth of adversity. Alfio is dissatisfied with his work on some shots, and so he's unhappy. Pino and the rest of the camera crew try their hardest to cheer up their boss. Aruna is upset about the gaps in continuity. Thierry has gone off the green walls in the hotel. Jean-Pierre Ruh is suffering on account of the traffic outside, which is spoiling his direct sound recordings. Everywhere there are difficulties, and people are wondering how to make it better. But with all that going on, I have the sense of a crew knitting together in adversity. I have to compliment Donata here: she's absolutely tireless in her efforts to restore morale. And I have to mention the heroic work of Judith, our make-up artist, and Fernando, the stylist and hairdresser. Those two are first on set in the morning, and last off it at night, without ever complaining; from the nature of their work, they need to dispense an awful lot of 'spiritual massage'. Over the past few days, I've seen practically everyone on the crew going in or out of their department, and I've noticed with wry pleasure that a good many of them are suddenly sporting some audacious new haircut, or some eyeliner or rouge. With every film there comes a moment when a new hairdo or a touch of make-up does wonders. I went in there myself today, and had Fernando's clippers cheer me up.

A production meeting is arranged, where all of us – the producers, Enrica, Beatrice, Alfio, etc. – talk over what we should do tomorrow. Much depends on whether Michelangelo will agree to depart from the chronological order, because otherwise we're threatened with losing a further whole day. Suggestions are put forward and alternatives aired, but much of it Michelangelo is unable to follow. This type of meeting can really only burden him, and he can't contribute much to it. He does seem to understand, though, that we won't be able to stick to our chronological order. It's decided that tomorrow we'll shoot the final scene of the first part of the episode, which has Silvano coming down the stairs into the lobby and trying to order some flowers from the manager. We've got the light for that all set up already.

We drive home through the fog in a pretty low state, depressed by the unsatisfactory rushes and by Michelangelo's physical condition. We should really try to keep these production decisions away from him, and let him conserve his energy for the actual shooting.

It's once more become apparent how great is Michelangelo's ability to live a scene when it's in front of him, and how little he can commit himself to it in advance; how difficult it is for him to answer our questions about it in an abstract way. He makes lots of sketches, but when we get to shooting the sketches are just paper and it's the actual conditions that count. Michelangelo's gift is to empathize and respond to the mood of a time and a place, not to preconceive these things from a script or from previously held ideas. For instance, we'd often love to know a day in advance where to position the cameras, but when we ask him his reply is always, 'No so!' In other words, 'How do you expect me to know that now?'

In the evening, my assistant Jolanda arrives from Berlin with a new stills camera for me. A couple of days ago Aruna knocked my Fuji 6 × 9 off a chair – accidentally, of course – and it's broken. Jolanda's also got the first contact sheets of the stills pictures from Portofino. I'm fairly pleased with the pictures, except I notice I don't always take enough time over them. But you're always under pressure when you're trying to take a few stills shots at the end of filming a scene. You can't do it beforehand, I think, because you'd break the concentration of the actors, and also because reconstructing a scene for a photographer is completely different from simulating it before it's been shot. Afterwards, there's generally the problem that work has to go on, and by taking pictures you're keeping people from taking down the lights, getting ready for the next scene, or even going for a bite of lunch.

It's not an easy job, and so, for a number of reasons, I've begun to take my own stills myself, as I have on my last few films. This way the actors aren't faced with a different pair of eyes after their scene; besides, as director you do have a little

53

more authority when it comes to getting people to give another minute of quiet and concentration. I've had interesting pictures from a number of stills photographers, but rarely, if ever, had pictures that were taken from the point of view of the film camera, and respected the cameraman's light. A lot of photographers, quite understandably, look for an angle of their own, and some different illumination, but I prefer those that show me what the film cameraman saw, and what the light was established to show.

FRIDAY 18.11.94   Thirteenth day of shoot

Just as well I'm not superstitious.

Today, for the first time, we have sunshine on our drive to Comacchio. In front of the hotel, as ever, a smile and a wave from Michelangelo, and then the two BMWs race in convoy through the flat Po Valley landscape.

On set, as discussed yesterday, Michelangelo finishes off the filming in the lobby. He wants to use all three cameras. *Tutto bene.* A couple of days ago we got a third camera, just to be on the safe side.

In the end we only use two. Silvano comes down the stairs, talks to the manager in the lobby, and orders a bowl of fruit for Carmen, because there are no flowers to be had. The shot ends, at my suggestion, with a close-up of the fruit. It's not the greatest idea ever, but because the scene goes straight into one of my linking sections, I wanted to have a little moment of calm to finish, so that I could tune in the voice of the 'director'.

In the afternoon we prepare, but don't shoot, the shots for Silvano's waking up, which actually precedes the scene in the lobby. Then we go with Michelangelo to look over a square in Comacchio: Treponti, as the name suggests, is a triple-arched bridge over a canal. It's a fantastic location that Michelangelo spotted by chance in the background on the documentary film crew's monitor. Enrica and Andrea filmed an interview with Tonino Guerra there. At any rate, Michelangelo saw it in the

Antonioni makes his point

shot as he went by, and straightaway wanted to film there – using it for the still outstanding scene of the first kiss between Carmen and Silvano. Originally, that was going to take place either at the end of the arcades, or else outside the hotel, but Michelangelo has quite spontaneously switched it to Comacchio. I'm absolutely with him, and am pleased that Michelangelo's film will thereby take in a bit of the surrounding scenery. Otherwise, the first half of the Ferrara episode would have taken place only in the hotel and under the arcades, and it might have felt a bit claustrophobic. I would have done exactly the same thing if I'd been in Michelangelo's situation, and that's what I tell the producers when they ask me anxiously what I think of such an impulsive departure from the screenplay. It's a decision that threatens to throw out our schedule a little further, but I back him up to the hilt. I'm full of admiration for the way he's managed to remain so flexible, even under all that pressure.

After the recce, during which Michelangelo once more absorbs a place with great intensity, I ask him whether he remembers it from the time he grew up in Ferrara. He gesticulates back: 'Of course I do . . .'

We need to take one more shot, namely the end of the arcade scene we had to break off yesterday when it got too dark. But as soon as we return to that location with Michelangelo, general panic breaks out. The sun didn't come back in the afternoon at all, so it won't get dark between quarter to five and five, as it did yesterday, but more like four o'clock. That leaves us with about fifteen minutes of light to capture the end of the scene. The water-wagon is sent out to sprinkle the street in the nick of time. The driver comes from a nearby village, and manages to do just about everything wrong. Yesterday his tanker – which was probably only half full to begin with – suddenly ran out of water, so we sat on helpless during the loveliest dusk, just waiting for him to fill up. We shoot without a run-through. At the last moment, Michelangelo plumps for a second camera after all, and in the midst of the ensuing chaos there's potential calamity: Pino is on the first, static, camera, while the second, which is to track and zoom, is suddenly in the hands of Carlo, whose handling of the zoom has proved less than satisfactory a couple of times already. I manage to swap them round in the nick of time, and get Pino on the more important camera.

And so we shoot, not into the dusk but rather at the tail end of it, especially with Alfio deciding, following the first take, that he needs to shed some more light on the whole scene. How all this is going to fit together with the footage we got yesterday is something of a mystery to me. Aruna, who's responsible for continuity, is tearing her hair out. On the other hand, Ines has got much better at her lines, and I think it's a great pity she can't have another crack at the whole of yesterday's dialogue scene. But that would mean another day lost, which would blow a huge hole in our schedule, so I button my lip. One way or another we get through the scene, though by the end it looks pretty black to me. Carmen and Silvano don't exchange their kiss, as per screenplay; instead it's saved for Treponti. As to when we'll get to film there, God only knows.

In the evening, Enrica leaves us for a couple of days' rest at the spa in Saturnia. She wants to get right away from the shoot, for which no one can blame her. With her two jobs – first, having to be available at all times to interpret and organize for Michelangelo, and secondly, being in charge of her documentary film crew – she has more on her plate than sometimes seems humanly possible. But she gets through it all, admirably and heroically. On the one hand, she's very much involved with Michelangelo's shoot – often enough she's right at the very heart of it – and the next minute she's having to be on the outside, observing it. In Agnes and Thomas she has a couple of ideal associates. Both of them have a fair measure of independence, Thomas with his Betacam, Agnes with the Super-8.

As Michelangelo's personal assistant, Andrea, is playing host to his parents this weekend, Michelangelo's support system has shrunk down to Giancarlo, his driver, and us. Donata and I have supper with him. Once more he's in a good mood, and when I get hiccups, he falls about laughing. Then I spill a glass of water all over my trousers and he laughs till he cries. Nothing I've done has ever tickled him as much as that bout of hiccups. At any rate, it seems to me that he has accepted me and my role a little, coming to view me not as a rival – which he occasionally did at the outset – but as an ally. Once more, I reassured him that he could rely on me to speak up for him, just as I would speak up for myself. He could depend on me to represent *his* interests, and not those of the producers, and I would do everything to see that he had the best possible conditions to work in. I'm convinced he believed me.

And yet he still seems worried that I might interfere with his work. For instance, when he sees me talking to the actors, he always keeps a beady eye on me. I try therefore to keep my communication with them on set to a bare minimum. In any case, it's generally to do with queries about the French or English text, or with interpreting his instructions.

This morning when we shot the scene with Silvano, the hotel manager and the fruit, Michelangelo and I decided after the first take that we needed the second camera too, whereupon I leapt up to give the instructions. But Michelangelo gripped my sleeve and said 'Aspetta!', possibly thinking I was going to determine the camera position at the same time. Of course I would never have done that. I've got in the habit of letting Michelangelo lead the way on to the set, and when there's a new camera placement to be discussed, I leave him alone with Alfio for a while, before joining them.

SATURDAY 19.11.94   Fourteenth day of shoot

It's only a half day today, because the Italian crew obviously think an early finish on Saturday is something Moses carried down with him from the Mount. It is, as they say, set in stone. Some of them want to get down to Rome to see their families. This half day finally makes it clear to the producers that we won't be moving across to Ferrara before Tuesday night. The only way we might have been able to finish on Monday is if we'd stayed up shooting half the night.

It's raining and feels chilly and damp, really unpleasant. We begin with the scene of Silvano waking up, which we discussed and lit yesterday evening. Once again, two cameras: one on a tripod, the other a Steadycam, following Silvano across the passage to Carmen's room, where he knocks on the door, and, not getting any reply, heads off down the stairs. Michelangelo has both cameras at wide angles, so their framing is rather similar, and we wonder how he'll manage to cut from one to the other. At first Alfio, then Pino, and then Beatrice and I try to persuade him to have one of them a bit tighter, at least to begin with, but Michelangelo stands firm. The argument that the two shot-sizes would be difficult to cut together interests him not at all. 'Niente!' is his unambiguous comment. Both cameras are to stay at long range, and to show 'Tutto!'

Enough time remains to shoot the first half of the scene where Carmen and Silvano return to the hotel. They walk upstairs, making small talk to hide their uncertainty about what might follow. Will he go to her room, are they going to sleep together?

The shot works very well, and if the Italian crew had been prepared to go on working, I'm sure we could have completed another couple of scenes. But that was never going to happen. It's OK really. If everybody carried on filming as maniacally as I sometimes wish, nobody would have any kind of home life at all. Giancarlo winks at me: 'Noi tedeschi mai stanchi . . .' It's become a kind of joke between us.

Michelangelo's editor, Claudio di Mauro, the subject of the dissension with the producers in Portofino, is visiting us today. As it's probably reached his ears that he wasn't instantly acceptable to everyone, his manner is correspondingly cagey, and he doesn't talk to anyone except Michelangelo. I can't say I blame him.

Today's rushes are mixed. The first part of the arcade scene is quite beautiful in places, but the best take with the Steadycam – in terms of acting, camerawork and lighting – has a huge scratch on the negative, and can't be used. The scene with Kim and Ines in the restaurant shows all of Ines's inexperience, and her difficulty with the language, but also how extremely photogenic she is, and a good editor should be able to make a decent scene out of the material.

Unfortunately there are also a couple of glaring lapses in continuity, and we wonder how they can be fudged. These things simply don't interest Michelangelo, but they'll annoy him later, at the editing table. We really should take him in hand a bit. But no one dares to say anything, least of all Aruna, whose job it is to avoid these mistakes, and who knows her business really. But she has been too often quelled by a brusque 'Via!' or 'Niente!' from Michelangelo.

There are a couple of framing mistakes in today's rushes too, and they are directly attributable to the religious way in which both Pino and Carlo follow Michelangelo's instructions, even when they can see with their own eyes that it would be better to leave out a piece of a chair on the left of the frame, or not to jam the actor right on the outer edge of the picture. Often enough, Michelangelo is in no position to judge these things on his snowy monitor. There are so many little imperfections that

The team huddle to peruse the monitor

provoke consternation during the rushes that could easily have been avoided if someone had shown a bit of courage during the filming. Because I'm watching most of the shots on the same monitor as Michelangelo there are a lot of things I haven't spotted either, because the picture quality on that thing is so wretched. It gives you a rough overall impression, but not these sort of details. There are far better video monitors on the market today, and it annoys me that this hugely important tool for Michelangelo has been scrimped on.

Michelangelo himself is only half-satisfied today, and when we ask him for his impression, he replies with 'Poco . . .' and a weighing movement of his hand that means 'so-so'. That evening, over supper in the hotel restaurant, he sketches the arcades again, and we try and guess what he's getting at, or maybe what he would like to shoot over again. But all he says to our suggested interpretations is 'forse . . .', which means: 'Maybe it would have been better that way, maybe not. We could have done it like this, but then again . . .'

One of the alternatives he sketches shows Carmen walking round the outside of a few pillars, slalom-fashion, followed by the camera, a bit like Sophie on the pier at Portofino. Or he draws Carmen and Silvano, not walking under the arcades at all, but down the street. As always, his drawings start off all manner of speculations. Are we going to re-shoot something? And if so, what?

Later, Michelangelo dances a slow waltz with Donata in the bar, then another with Jolanda, and he's in great spirits again; while the rest of us are collapsing with fatigue, he's brimming with energy.

With all the problems that crop up, with all the differences of opinion on set and all the difficulties Michelangelo occasionally plunges us into, there isn't a single one of us who wouldn't forgive him everything for a single smile. For the way he overcomes his handicap, and slowly but surely gives this film its form, and each scene his unmistakable stamp, he wins the respect of each and every one of us. Michelangelo can be very hard, and sometimes hurtful, but then he's not soft on himself either. I remember one often-quoted sentence of his – who knows when he said it? – 'Living for me means one thing: making films.' He demonstrates that to us, in such a way that it applies to all of us too, at least for the duration of this film. And I might be mistaken, but it seems to me that Michelangelo's vocabulary is growing along with the film!

SUNDAY 20.11.94   Rest day

A chance to sleep in. Of course I wake up promptly at seven, but I read for half an hour, and drop off again. My dreams are more vivid than they've been in a long time.

At lunchtime I've an interview with a professor from Milan who's gone through *Wings of Desire* frame by frame with her class, over several weeks. Her questions are of a highly philosophical nature, and it's difficult for me, in the middle of a new film, to find my way back into an old one. There's much mention of Heidegger and psychoanalysis, and I need to really make an effort to say anything halfway sensible. When you make a film, you do it as much with your heart and with gut instinct as with your brain. I do anyway.

Michelangelo wants to go to the cinema – something that was mentioned last night – but Donata and I honestly don't have the time. We need to choose pictures with Jolanda from the new contact sheets she brought with her, and I want to get on with my diary. So Michelangelo heads off with Stephane, Felice and Andrea in tow. They've decided to see Benigni's *Il mostro*.

In the evening we show Michelangelo the first prints of our pictures from Portofino. He's really quite a merciless critic, and even tears up a few where he doesn't like himself, before we can stop him. We're a little shocked at his ferocity, and his lack of courtesy. It's not really about the pictures either, it's more that Michelangelo wants to show who's in charge, because, a little later, looking over the pictures of the Sygma photographer Richard Melloul, who was with us in Portofino for a few days, Michelangelo allows them all to pass, even some he would have torn up if they'd been ours.

Then a meeting with Philippe, Stephane and Felice. At issue is the slow pace of the filming, and ways in which it might be stepped up. Alfio seems too slow to them, and so does the entire camera department. I agree only up to a point. Alfio's experience of Michelangelo has made him cautious, because of the way he makes his decisions on the spot. That means he can't really prepare even the littlest thing ahead of Michelangelo's decision. Also, he needs time because Michelangelo generally starts off with an establishing shot that shows everything. 'Tutto!' On top of that, it's very tricky to set a halfway decent light for two cameras filming in tandem. Given all that, you really can't accuse Alfio of being slow.

MONDAY 21.11.94   Fifteenth day of shoot

We've a lot on today, three set-ups in all: the other part of the scene on the stairs, showing Carmen and Silvano reaching the first-floor landing, and him asking her which room is hers, then the two of them going into their rooms, then each of them alone, waiting for the other.

When Michelangelo turns up in the morning, we feel something's amiss. He looks tense and drawn, seems out of sorts, barely says hello, and goes straight up to the first location, which is Silvano's room. There he promptly throws a fit because he's required to film it in the daytime, when it says night in the script. He must have forgotten what we decided at the end of last night's discussion, when we had to agree to that little concession. We've seen Silvano's room by day, when he wakes up in the morning scene, which had the windows in shot, the view out on to the street and the landscape beyond. Because today's action is all between the bed and the door, and therefore can only be filmed from the other, window, side of the room, the windows themselves won't be in shot, so it won't hurt if they're blacked out, and we film 'day for night'. Alfio and Andrea, with honeyed tongues, manage to talk Michelangelo round.

Once he's fixed the positions of the two cameras, it turns out that the windows are, and indeed can only be, out of shot. The filming with Kim is very swift, because he's as precise as he always is. Michelangelo's mood persists, however. Today I'm in the line of fire. As always, I'm sitting beside him in front of the two monitors, squeezed into the corner on top of a camera battery, but each time the second camera pans, I'm forced over towards Michelangelo. I press against him ever so slightly, but straightaway I get a jab in the ribs and a disgusted-looking expression: 'Keep away from me, you!' The whole thing isn't without its comic side, because the scene with Kim needs to be taken several times, so I need to take evasive action from the camera each time, and each time I catch an elbow in the ribs. Pino, who's manning the camera, is doubled up with laughter; he's the only one who's seen our little Laurel and Hardy number. The electrician outside the window is supposed to create the light effect of a car passing outside, but he isn't up to it, and keeps beaming his light on the ceiling, where neither of the cameras can catch it. The whole thing has to be done over and over again. It's ghastly.

Much later than planned we go on to the next set-up, which is the other part of the scene on the landing. Yesterday Michelangelo suggested a couple of camera positions which would have captured the scene perfectly, but it's not his day today. He sticks with the positions, but switches the cameras round. So Pino now finds himself doing a static master, and can switch off halfway through the scene because the actors have walked out of shot, whereas the less experienced Carlo has to do the more complicated job of panning round with long focal length and zoom full out. Not surprisingly, the scene needs to be retaken a few times. Another consequence of the camera switch is that Carmen and Silvano seem to be looking past each other; they're almost in profile. With the cameras as they were yesterday, they would have been in half-profile shots, and much better. Michelangelo has fallen into a trap of his own making, and has only himself and his bad mood to blame for the fact that no one will come forward and help him out of it. Not even me. I got shouted at during the first run-through of the scene. 'Zitto!' ('Shut up!') he snarls, even though all I was doing was conveying his instructions to the actors in English or French. Finally, having got a solid blow with his left hand, like Andrea, Enrica and a few others before me, I stalk off set. This job isn't worth getting knocked around for. So I sit and lick my wounds in the lobby downstairs, and decide to let Michelangelo stew in his own juice for today.

But I can't keep it up for very long, because Andrea comes down and asks me, on behalf of Michelangelo, to come back. They are ready upstairs. So I'm back on board, but I take Donata's advice and begin by giving Michelangelo one back, which he takes with some glee, and hits me again. With that ritual exchange over, we're pals again, both grinning from ear to ear. It's hard to be angry with Michelangelo for long, especially when he looks at you guiltily with his sad eyes. There's no way of resisting that look. And when I think how I would go crazy if, like him, I could sort everything out in my head, and not be able to communicate any of it, then I have to forgive him his

Intimacy: Kim Rossi-Stuart and Ines Sastres

'Vias!' and 'Fuoris!' and 'Nientes!', as well as the occasional blow. Precisely when you think his mood will never lift he gives you a smile or a gesture to show that he's taking an ironic view of the thing again.

Once the second set-up – with Carlo on the problematic camera – has finally been finished without any glitches, it's already suppertime. My suggestion that we wrap for the day isn't taken seriously, because everyone hopes that by two a.m. the day's third scene might be in the bag as well. That way, we could strike the set by noon tomorrow, and we could go on to the kiss scene at Treponti in the afternoon.

Fat chance. By the time we've finished the long scene with Ines in her room, it's way past four a.m. She's extremely nervous about appearing naked, and in the end she's only prepared to expose her breast briefly in half-profile as she pulls on her nightdress. I'm impressed with the resolve with which she opposes Michelangelo's further demands. Finally, after watching the scene on the monitor with me and Michelangelo, she asks for one more take. She's allowed it, and it's easily her best: it has a lovely flowing movement from beginning to end. However, it's impossibly late by now, and the upshot of that is that we'll only be able to strike the set; there's no time for the kiss scene at Treponti. And the knock-on effect of that is that Treponti has to be postponed until after the filming in Ferrara. Because if we shoot nothing tomorrow, and only the bit with the kiss on the day after, that would put us fully four days behind schedule. So we decide to strike the hotel set tomorrow, and light the cinema in Ferrara, our next location. That way, at least the cinema scene can be done, as per schedule, on the day after tomorrow.

Bushed by the usual half-hour's drive through the fog, we're back at the 'Duchessa Isabella' at five in the morning. Michelangelo is also very tired, but he remained awake right through this night shoot. When I point out that we won't be getting much sleep tonight he gives me to understand that he never sleeps much. And what does he do with his sleepless nights? Michelangelo points to the television, and shrugs.

TUESDAY 22.11.94   Rest and removal day

I wake up after three hours, and can't get back to sleep. I was dreaming of the shoot, compulsively going through the same situation over and over again. Yesterday's conflict with Michelangelo is preying on my mind. Dreaming and half-awake, I kept going back to his rough and sometimes offensive manner, and my attempts to convince him that we couldn't help him if he wouldn't let us.

During the day I work for a couple of hours with Uli Felsberg, the managing director of Road Movies. There are contracts and financial arrangements to think about. He's going back to Berlin tomorrow, and today's our last chance to sort these things out.

I press Enrica to persuade Michelangelo to shoot out of sequence tomorrow, doing the scene outside the cinema first and the one inside later. If we manage them both, it will mean we've made up half a day. It seems worth the attempt anyway. The producers have threatened to cancel the 'Due telefaxi' episode if we're more than three or four days behind when we finish in Aix-en-Provence. They're pretty pessimistic about the prospects for the shoot – understandable after the past week here – and are trying to come up with ways of speeding things up. I point out that from the beginning we've never been able to shoot more than two set-ups a day – three or four shots, five at the most – and that we need to stick to what is evidently Michelangelo's tempo, not only for the sake of the budget, but so that a good film gets made. It's only at this pace that Michelangelo can really control the film, and that, after all, is what our aim has been all along.

I have to be careful not to get too involved in the producers' arguments, so that I can keep my credibility with Michelangelo as his partner, back-up man and rearguard. He's inclined to suspect conspiracies anyway. That's probably been his experience with producers all his life. He's never produced himself, as I have from the beginning; all his life he's been a hired hand, forced to fight for his freedom and his authorship, always up against the conditions producers have tried to lay down.

WEDNESDAY 23.11.94 Sixteenth day of shoot

It takes us all morning to get a pretty straightforward shot in the big courtyard of the old Piazza del Municipio. We're stalled for a start because the costumes for the second half of the Ferrara story, 'three years later', haven't been chosen yet, and the actors have to show Michelangelo all the various possibilities and permutations. That makes them late for their make-up, and the start of filming is accordingly held up. The camera's ready and a tracking shot has been prepared with the crane, but Michelangelo has to sit in the cold for two hours doing nothing, surrounded by many hundreds of gawping onlookers. At last we're ready.

Michelangelo surprises us by indicating that for once the camera isn't going to be on Carmen, as we had automatically assumed after the first weeks of filming, but it is to follow Silvano. For the first time he allows the female figure to walk out of the picture entirely. And then we're further confused because, according to Michelangelo's instructions, the story is going to be slightly different from the way it is in the script. We'd assumed that Silvano must have seen Carmen in the cinema, but the way Michelangelo is now directing it, Silvano seems to just bump into her outside after the film.

The second camera is positioned parallel to the first one, and its framing is broadly the same. Twice I tell Carlo to go for some more width, but he sticks rigidly to what he thinks Michelangelo's instructions have been. Unfortunately that obedience, as we've seen in the rushes, can have bad results. This is another one of these shots on the second camera when the actors will be up against the edge of the frame, and clumsily hacked-off bits of architectural detail will disfigure the overall picture. Michelangelo can't see that on his monitor, but when you look through the lens it's clear enough. The next lot of rushes will have him tearing his hair out, I can see it coming. But I'm up against a brick wall.

Because there's so little activity I take more photographs than usual, and, unusually for me, some shots behind the camera. I've been asked to take a few pictures for the city council, to show the filming taking place against the backdrop of the town hall. At last I can take out the panorama camera, which will do justice to the proportions of this beautiful Renaissance courtyard.

Michelangelo's brother Alberto has come to visit him, and it's quite touching to see the two old men, wrapped in their winter coats, sitting together in the middle of the courtyard, watching the goings-on on their monitors. I suspect Michelangelo also enjoys the crowds, who are watching everything he does.

When lunch comes we think we've done the scene with the two camera positions, but no, it seems there's more to come. But what? There's no time to stand around guessing. There's enough light left for one more shot, and that's going to be of Silvano walking down the cinema steps and going out on to the forecourt. Carmen is there in the background with her friend Sara. Because we're still not certain whether Silvano has already spotted Carmen in the cinema or whether he first caught sight of her this minute, Kim cleverly plays the scene in an open way that doesn't rule out either possibility. Sometimes Michelangelo answers us with 'Si', sometimes it's 'No'. Our lesson from that is that we should have anchored this day in the chronology of the narrative. Then we would know whether it was 'Si' or 'No'. I'm sorry now that I supported the suggestion of departing from chronological order, especially as the day's gone so badly that we haven't made up any ground. We might as well have shot in sequence, and begun indoors.

The evening's rushes are once again a curate's egg. The scenes with Carmen and Silvano alone in their respective rooms are OK, but the entire arcade scene is very variable. God knows whether all the differences in light and mood and picture quality will allow for convincing editing. The second camera seems increasingly inadequate, and its value seems more and more doubtful to me. It's only in the Steadycam sequences that it pays its way at all; apart from that, I think we would be better off without it.

In the end I come out feeling disappointed by the rushes, and I'm probably not the only one. Michelangelo seems to have less of a feeling for this story than he did for the first one in Portofino. He hasn't really clicked with his two young principals, and with the relationship they're supposed to have. In a lot of the footage the framing is too wide, in others it's too tight. In Portofino there didn't seem to be that sort of indeterminacy. Enrica agrees when I talk to her about it. It was partly on my recommendation that the Ferrara story was adopted for the script, because I thought it was so typical of Michelangelo. Also, the producers were dead set on having the maestro filming in his native city, not least so that the framing narrative could also be set here, and thus be connected to the rest of the film. Once again, I feel I would have done better to keep my mouth shut. Michelangelo was much more familiar with the other three episodes, which he had been carrying around with him as possible film ideas for many years. Tonino had already dramatized and scripted them many times over. 'Cronaca di un amore mai esistito' was perhaps adopted too quickly for Michelangelo to really make it his own, as he had the other stories.

Over supper I try to persuade Michelangelo that we can only help him if we're kept better informed about his intentions. But that conversation soon hits the buffers. Michelangelo points to himself: 'Io', which might mean 'I can do it', or 'I know what I'm doing', or, when he's furious, 'Leave me alone, I know what I want.' Today's 'Io' seems a bit more uncertain, and he points to his mouth: 'Parlare.' But whether he would confide in us much more if he had been able to speak, even Enrica has her doubts. He has never been one for big pronouncements before a shot, and has always kept his cards fairly close to his chest, so as to be able to adapt and change with the circumstances. That makes my task – and, in fact, all of our tasks – an exercise in patience.

So that little initiative of mine misfires, and when I show him a drawing, to help us discuss tomorrow's extra shot (for which Tonino has in the meantime written some lines of dialogue), so we can at least figure out what might be in shot and where we can park our trucks and the big generator, he puts an end to the conversation: 'No so!' He doesn't know where he's going to put the camera. God knows, I can readily identify with that, but it will create further delays. We're almost a week behind, and if we carry on like this, the producers will be unable to finance the fourth episode in Paris. That would be a terrible shame, because I think 'Due telefaxi' is actually the most exciting of all four episodes, on paper anyway, and I hope with all my heart that he'll be allowed to shoot that story set among the skyscrapers of La Défense.

Thursday 24.11.94 Seventeenth day of shoot

After yesterday, when everything passed off so grimly and the crew was completely listless, I'd decided to approach my task more in the manner of an American first assistant, and create a bit of urgency on set. And today that's what I did. I was on set half an hour early, I went through the day's shooting plan with Beatrice, and, with the help of the little Hi-8 Viewcam, made a kind of demo with the actors to show Michelangelo what the Steadycam would make of the proposed walk past the basilica. Yesterday, he'd intimated that he wanted to use the mobile camera for that.

Then when he comes, I'm actually rather relieved – considering past experience – that he doesn't even want to look at our tape, but instead has some tracks laid down right away. In view of all the right angles on the buildings and the cathedral in the background, I'm sure that's a better choice than the moving camera. Michelangelo also knows exactly where he wants the actors to walk. Only, against the advice of the camera crew, he has the rails laid down the street, and not on the pavement. That way, it takes the 18 mm wide-angle lens to get the whole of the cathedral in shot, which in turn means the actors' faces are pretty warped. I hope it doesn't look too bad on the rushes. But then he does another take afterwards using a longer focal length, which gives him another option.

After that, he wants to get the eerie, almost De Chirico-like castle of Ferrara into shot, so he adds a shot showing Silvano and Carmen from behind, carrying on where the previous one left off. That, too, is filmed on tracks, and is quickly done. It's good for the crew to be under pressure. Beatrice has the traffic, the pedestrians and the innumerable cyclists well in hand, and we have three shots in the bag before lunch. That's three times as much as we managed in the whole of yesterday!

In the cinema in the afternoon, Michelangelo pulls off three more really lovely shots, and one astonishing bit of shooting. The last of the shots, which needs terrific depth of focus so that

Alfio has to build up the lighting in the cinema to 'Level 8', seems especially wonderful. Carmen and her friend Sara get up and leave the cinema at the end of the film. But as they leave shot, we see Silvano in the background, sitting up in the circle. He hasn't seen them. After a while he also gets up to leave. Thanks to the depth of focus, the scene has an unexpected resolution. Now, we finally understand what was on Michelangelo's mind yesterday when he filmed the reunion – not as scripted – showing Silvano seeing the girl outside the cinema for the first time. Thank God Kim played the scene so ambivalently that it worked either way. If we had fouled that up, it would have been my fault, because it was only in response to my incessant questions – had Silvano seen her inside or not? – that Michelangelo's 'No' had become a 'Si'. So if we'd followed Michelangelo's instructions, the other way – this new way – wouldn't have been possible. But because he has to rely so often on the small screen – which doesn't show the details of a performance at all – I'd become uncertain about what was supposed to have happened in the cinema. And all that turned out for the best in today's shoot. Michelangelo has got a firm hold on his story, and is directing with fresh confidence.

There's only a momentary crisis when we rehearse the house lights going up at the end of the film. Vehement protests from Michelangelo. He makes this strange hissing noise, and says something about the lights. But what? Does he want them on quicker? No, it's not that. Does he want the neon lights on as well? No, not that either. We're stumped, and Michelangelo is frustrated. Finally he sketches the screen and a projector beam in his notepad. Ah, does he want the projector light to be discernible in the cinema? For a while that's how it appears, and we try to talk him out of it. You can't project the film on the screen and throw rays of bright light on it at the same time. It would only work in countershot. We could create a bit of haze in the cinema, then the actual beam from the projector might show up against it. But it's not that easy, because then our own lights would become visible as well, and Alfio would have to relight the entire scene. It would take hours. But then it seems that wasn't what Michelangelo was after either. After a long debate, we return to our original version. And that now seems to be fine for Michelangelo. Sometimes he starts protesting wildly, but it's only some tiny detail that's bothering him. We all go around thinking of sweeping alterations, but he only wants some small adjustment, like the other day, when it turned out that his drastic protest was only to do with Ines's coat flapping open, or a turn of the head being to the left instead of the right. With little things, his reactions are sometimes vehement, whereas major alterations are allowed to go through without demur.

It's becoming ever clearer to me that this episode in Ferrara, the way it's emerging, will require a different framing narrative from me than the one I'd envisaged. What we're filming here seems to me altogether dreamier and more unreal than the Portofino story, which was far more physical and direct. The wide long shots and extreme close-ups, the breaks of continuity, the light, the colours, the fog – in a word, the whole atmosphere of the story – could well work as a dream on the part of the 'director', whereas the Portofino story seems more like something 'imagined' or 'contrived' by him.

Perhaps I should do something to establish the two actors, Ines and Kim, in my narrative in some way that would justify the casting of such a youthful pair in Michelangelo's story. Maybe, just thinking aloud now, I could actually show Ines as a model, or being discovered by the 'director' in a fashion magazine, the way Michelangelo actually came across Ines Sastre.

Anyway, I'm looking forward more and more to my two weeks in February, when I get to shoot. Whether Michelangelo's preferred choice, Daniel Day-Lewis, is actually going to play the 'director' seems rather doubtful at the moment. From what I'm hearing, it sounds as though I'll have to look around for another possibility. Michelangelo himself recently mentioned Gian-Maria Volonte again. He was my first casting idea for the part, but Michelangelo turned him down for the role of 'himself', as it were. But now it seems important to me that an older actor plays the 'director', especially as you can see from Michelangelo's own episodes that they are not the product of a youthful imagination, but made by a mature man. By casting the 'director' well, I can actually strengthen the integration of Michelangelo's episodes into the film as a whole. What if I used John Malkovich? That had been my assumption for a while, that the 'director' in my framework would be the same as the main actor in the Portofino episode, but after a while we got away from that again.

Irene Jacob is here on a visit, to try out costumes and make-up. She's looking forward to her filming; her joy shows in her face. *Victory*, the film she's been making for Mark Peploe, is finished, and over supper she tells us enthusiastically about working with Willem Dafoe. Michelangelo pricks up his ears. Willem had once been his ideal casting for 'Due telefaxi', and with that episode now pushed back to the beginning of next year, he wants to know whether there's any chance that he'll be available then.

I catch Willem in New York. He picks up the phone himself. Yes, he's available from the end of February, and he says: 'I'm game. If Michelangelo wants me, I'd like to be part of it. Count me in.' It's Thanksgiving in America, and he's just putting the turkey in the oven. He'd have to say his lines in French, of course. 'Pas de problème,' he says suavely.

Michelangelo is delighted. It really would be great if Willem could join us.

On MTV they're showing the European Music Awards in front of the Brandenburg Gate in Berlin. My U2 clip of *Faraway, So Close* has been nominated for it. But unfortunately (or should I say thank God?) the hotel doesn't pick up MTV, and I only hear later on the telephone that we didn't win. Just as well, really.

FRIDAY 25.11.94   Eighteenth day of shoot

This evening Donata and I have to fly to Berlin. I'm still the chairman of the European Film Academy, which is having a plenary session, and then there's the awarding of the European Film Prize.

Today the crew is settling into the beautiful old palazzo, where Carmen's apartment will be filmed over the next three or four days. The building is in the old town centre, right opposite the famous Palazzo Diamante. It's a wonderful location, featuring a huge pillared courtyard. Michelangelo is rigging up a complicated crane shot for the arrival of Carmen and Silvano. It demands a lot from us all, but everyone's up for it and works with a will.

It takes a while, once more, to find out just what crane and camera movements Michelangelo has in mind, but finally we're there. I think it's an excellent shot. I get the sense that Michelangelo is much more on top of things here in Ferrara than he was out in Comacchio. My job is increasingly being whittled down to co-ordinating the work, and communicating Michelangelo's intentions to the others. I'm particularly concerned to keep up the faster pace of the filming. Apart from that, Michelangelo needs me less than he did at the start. There are far fewer reasons to intervene or to make suggestions. I won't worry about the filming tomorrow, in my absence.

Irene tries out her costume and make-up. The suggested look makes her appear rather old, almost as though she's already taken the veil! She needs to look more youthful and fun-loving, so that her part can be as surprising as it is in the script. The brownish tints and the faded blue of her dress make her seem rather unworldly and almost 'backwoodsy'. Esther and Irene are going to Paris over the weekend to keep looking for costumes.

I'm still there for the first discussion of the dialogue scene between Carmen and Silvano in her apartment, which is going to be filmed tomorrow. Then we say our goodbyes, go back to the hotel, quickly pack our bags, and drive out to the airport in Bologna.

We fly, via Frankfurt, to Berlin and arrive late. Then straight into a taxi to the processing lab in Neukölln, where the grader's been waiting for us, to carry out the first colour- and light-grading on *Lisbon Story*. Lisa Rinzler, the camerawoman, is away on another shoot, and this is my only chance of influencing the print that's going to be shown in Lisbon in two weeks' time.

The silent print is consistently too bright, and the whole thing seems rather lumpy. I have a hard time getting back into the film. Of course, there's no soundtrack at all – no dialogue or music or original sound of any kind. It's almost two a.m. when we finally leave the lab and go home.

SATURDAY 26.11.94   Nineteenth day of shoot

Back in Ferrara – though I only get to hear about it from Beatrice on the telephone – Michelangelo filmed the whole long dialogue scene in Carmen's apartment in one shot, without a cut, even if it did take them twenty takes! That was the day's work. It seems to have gone very well.

My programme today in Berlin: first the press conference for this year's 'Felix' awards, then a meeting with Aina Bellis, the general secretary of the European Film Academy, then a trip to the cinema to see Gianni Amelio's *L'America*, and then the vote by Academy members. I'll only vote for the 'European film of the year', as I haven't been able to see the three debut films that were listed in that category. Then the plenary meeting. There are over forty members of the Academy present. Jack Lang gives a speech in which he urges the setting aside of a certain percentage of the European Structural Fund to benefit European cinema. It's followed by a lively discussion, with interesting contributions from Jim Sheridan, Agnieszka Holland and Michel Piccoli.

I really ought to write my speech for tomorrow's prizegiving, but I'm too tired, and decide to get up early and do it in the morning instead.

Sunday 27.11.94   Rest day

It may be a rest day in Ferrara, but not here in Berlin, on this first Sunday of Advent. I write out my speech for the prizegiving, which is taking place later this morning. Last year Antonioni was our guest of honour at the award ceremony, where he was given the Lifetime Achievement Award by the Academy. We were in the early stages of script meetings then, and our film was still a remote project.

Max von Sydow performs the duties of emcee with characteristic charm and dignity. This year's rather improvised Felix ceremony in a mirrored tent ends up being praised by all the participants; some even preferred it to the more elaborate ceremonies of past years.

There follows a symposium on the subject of remakes. Arthur Hiller (the president of the American Academy), Jean-Jacques Beneix and Nick Powell are among the participants. The whole thing would have been pretty tedious without the shouted interjections of Chantal Ackerman from the floor.

And then the first session of the new committee, unfortunately without Ettore Scola, Tilda Swinton and Ben Kingsley, all of whom are away filming, but with a lot of new impetus from Beneix, who has just been taken on board. Then, as ever, people start drifting off to catch their planes and we end up having failed to make some important decisions, notably on the future of the 'Felix' and the future site of the Academy. It's too early to say whether the idea of Strasbourg will come to anything. Stockholm is a possibility too, and so is North Rhine Westphalia.

Then supper, in honour of our American guest Arthur Hiller, with those Academy members who are still present, and then home, and another round of packing.

Monday 28.11.94   Twentieth day of shoot

Get up at half past four. As I'd already feared yesterday, I've come down with something. Sore throat, pain behind my eyes, joint pains, etc.

We fly anyway, via Frankfurt, to Bologna. Bad pain in my ears on landing, and when we get to Comacchio, it's obvious I need to go to bed. We drop in on the shoot on the way. Michelangelo is just filming the scene where Silvano leaves Carmen's apartment, then stops halfway down the long passage and turns back. A set of tracks and two static cameras have been set up. Michelangelo is firing on all cylinders. He's sitting behind his – three of them now – monitors, and seems more focused than ever. When we arrive we get just a smile and a brief hello, and then it's straight back to work. Actually, this is exactly the situation we'd dreamed of, with him able to film on his own, and me on standby, just in case. And now it's really happening. I can take to my bed without worrying.

By now I've got a temperature. The doctor sent for by the production office, not least for insurance reasons, comes with an empty bag. He's left everything behind, including his stethoscope. So he puts his ear to my chest, where he claims to hear a rattle. He doesn't have the torch to shine down my throat, but he still announces that everything's inflamed, and prescribes a course of antibiotics. At least he's remembered his prescription pad, but I suspect it's probably just so I can autograph it for his little girl. *Bene.*

After the wrap, Beatrice reports that Michelangelo has completed today's schedule without any difficulties. I'm completely exhausted, and sleep till morning.

Tuesday 29.11.94   Twenty-first day of shoot

I don't feel up to much in the morning, but at least my temperature's dropped. I seem to have given the bug to Donata, though. There are others who haven't managed to escape it either. Jean-Pierre has been recording the sound for days with blocked ears and a bunged-up nose. Everywhere there are red eyes and runny noses, coughs and splutters. Despite our ill health we drive down to the set a little later, just in time to catch the first shot. Silvano comes out of the building, goes round the corner, and walks along the edge of the building, to a point where the camera pans up and discovers Carmen at the window, watching him go.

The second shot is off a big crane. There's a certain amount of confusion as to the movement, but I'm able to clear it up. The scene is very beautiful. Michelangelo does have a penchant for these 'big shots'; for this one, he's had half the town blocked off, and the streets have been cleared of cars for hundreds of yards. Once again, he seems thoroughly alert and on the ball, completely different from the way he was during the first couple of weeks.

I'm delighted that I can take a couple of stills with the Palazzo Diamante in the background, but at lunchtime Donata and I head back to the hotel for more rest. We're just not well enough to work, and if we don't go to bed for a while, we'll just lose more time later on.

Towards evening, we watch a demo-tape of a 'Camera Zeppelin', a hot-air balloon with a remote-control camera fitted to it. Michelangelo is thinking of using it for the shot in the church in Aix. It's quite a big, clumsy thing, but it seems to work – at least on the demo-tape it does. It really could be interesting – I'm thinking of the scene where Niccolo falls asleep in the church. I'm going to talk to the inventor tomorrow, to find out how practical this flying monster really is.

There's some good news from Paris: it appears we will be able to film 'Due telefaxi' in the twin towers of the Société Générale in La Défense after all, but only in the second and third weeks of February. That means that my own shoot will now be put back until the beginning of March.

This evening, it's also decided that we're going to move on to Aix-en-Provence tomorrow, after all. The one missing scene in Comacchio, the kiss at Treponti, can be filmed while I'm shooting my own story there in March. Last week, at the height of the calamitous delays, I suggested to the producers that I give Michelangelo one of my own days. That would enable him to shoot his missing kiss, if he still wanted it, and to finish off the arcade scene. I'm fairly sure that when he's made his rough-cut, he'll see that he does need both those things. There was some muttering yesterday that he might drop the kiss.

That will give us a chance to shoot a scene with Michelangelo himself in it – if he's agreeable, that is. I'm really quite drawn to the idea, and Michelangelo has more than once agreed to do it. I think his image has to come up in my part of the film, but in such a way that his handicapped speech and movement don't appear. Only today, in Agnes's Super-8 films, we saw what an impressive figure he makes when he's standing off somewhere by himself, instead of leaning on someone's arm.

That Super-8 film which Agnes is shooting more or less off her own bat is really turning out beautifully, if you can tell on the basis of the twenty three-minute rolls that have been shot so far. The pictures radiate strength in a way that video images of the same scenes simply wouldn't. With the absence of sound, it really doesn't show that Michelangelo can't talk – in fact he communicates powerfully in them. With his gestures and hand movements, he is really the master of this film. Even uncut, the footage makes a wonderful document of this shoot. I hope it can remain pure, and not have to be 'stepped on' with video.

WEDNESDAY 30.11.94
Twenty-second day of shoot and travelling day

This morning my sore throat is worse, but the temperature's gone, and I feel better in myself.

Michelangelo is filming the love scene between Silvano and Carmen, with two cameras of course. Ines appears to have finally agreed to appear naked, or in her knickers. The actors are both very good. Michelangelo gives precise instructions about movements and gestures. In the equivalent scene in Portofino he was much less 'eloquent' and exact than he is now. He really does seem to be transformed; two weeks ago, none of us would have dreamed that he would be such a powerful and commanding presence on set.

We're through by lunch. There's departure in the air. Some are staying behind, like the Italian ladies on the production staff: Loretta, Ornella, Loredana and Christiana. But Carlo, the second cameraman and Steadycam operator, isn't coming with us either. In Aix, the crew will be joined instead by cameraman Jörg Widmer, who, in view of all the walks through the city and the heavy workload that that entails, will be of inestimable value to us. Certainly, Carlo didn't disgrace himself on the Steadycam, but Jörg is really one of the best cameramen in the world.

The bulk of the team aren't leaving till tomorrow, as things still need to be dismantled here in Ferrara. Tomorrow we're going to walk around the old centre of Aix with Michelangelo, to see if any of our fourteen designated locations can be amalgamated or perhaps dropped, which, according to Beatrice, needs to happen if we're to have any chance of keeping up with our schedule.

Because Donata and I feel too unwell to drive ourselves, Yorick, the French stage manager, drives us. We sit in the back and discuss my framework.

How can it best lend support to Michelangelo's episodes? It mustn't draw too much attention to itself. But at the same time it should establish its own identity. It should provide continuity, but not so much suspense that the stories, when they come, are felt to be an interruption or a distraction (that would be a disaster). Nor do I want my framework to get too dark, too heavy, or too dull.

Maybe our 'director' ought to meet the characters in Michelangelo's episodes, and be more involved with them than we presently imagine. As of now, he's still a rather nebulous, ascetic figure. Maybe he should get involved with a woman, given that that's what happens in all four of Michelangelo's stories. It needn't be wildly erotic . . .

At any rate, this framing action still contains a lot of exciting, unexplored story material that I need to dig up.

We reach Aix late in the evening, check into the hotel, and collapse into bed.

THURSDAY 1.12.94 Rest and preparation day

I feel really terrible this morning, so we call another doctor. This one comes fully equipped. He sees extensive inflammation in my throat – which ought to have improved after three days of antibiotics – and he advises me to carry on with a different one, with some cortisone as well for good measure.

We walk around the old city with Michelangelo, looking at the locations for the long walk of Niccolo and 'the girl', as she's referred to in the script. We're going to do the filming half in the daytime, half at night, with a long scene in a church in between. It really is a wonderfully pretty place, and all the locations are very attractive. I'm sure there are a couple of street locations too many, but it feels hard to drop any of them. Michelangelo has put together a very pleasing itinerary here.

The thirteenth-century church, St Jean de Malte, is very beautiful inside, notably plain and unadorned for a Catholic church. The day before yesterday we saw the demo-tape of the Zeppelin camera, and now we wonder, in situ, whether a flying camera with a maximum of two and a half minutes of film would be useful here, or if we're not just letting ourselves in for a very time-consuming adventure if we get the inventor and his four-man crew up from Rome. The precedent of the helicopter camera in *Faraway, So Close* is rather discouraging, because a lot of money and time didn't result in a great deal in the end.

There is a good atmosphere. Now that we've left the rather oppressive fogs of Ferrara behind, and are in the bright and welcoming city of Aix, everyone is in a better mood. Irene and Vincent are cheerful and energetic, and it's a real pleasure to watch the pair of them walking down the street together, practising their lines. Michelangelo is still a bundle of energy and full of creativity. I have great hopes for this episode; I think it's the best one in terms of script, actors and locations.

Donata and I now wonder whether it's right to shoot the whole of my part in Ferrara. It would be possible to shoot the links for the first two of Michelangelo's stories in Ferrara and

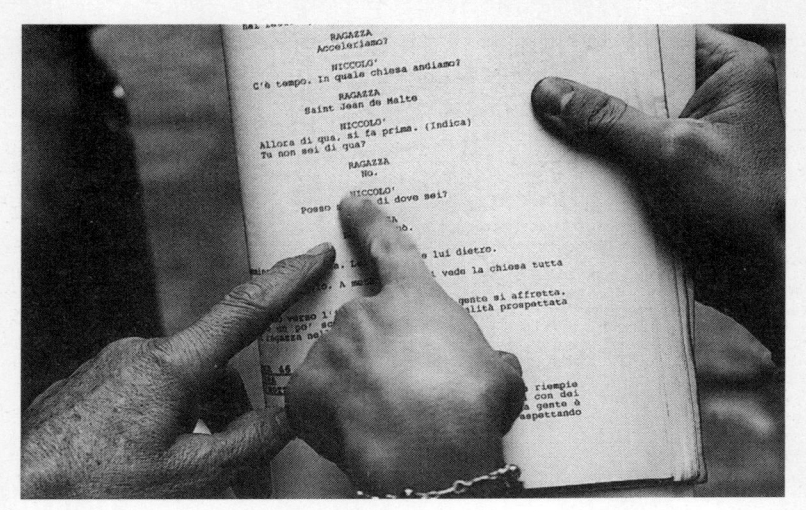

Pointing out the finer points of dialogue

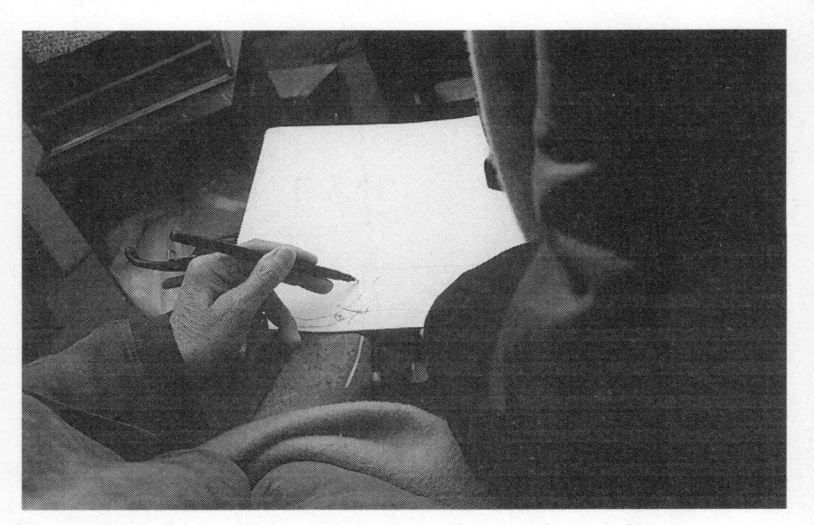

Antonioni finds an artful way to explain what's on his mind . . .

Comacchio, and then move on to Aix for the last two. That would make sense, not least as those third and fourth episodes both play in France. Tempting.

Friday 2.12.94   Twenty-third day of shoot

We approach this episode perfectly chronologically, beginning with the very first shot: a chance meeting between Niccolo and the girl in a doorway. But, in contradiction to what he said yesterday, Michelangelo wants to begin with both cameras outside – yesterday there was to be one outside and one inside, then both of them inside. Today they're both outside, which is a shame, not just because Thierry has put a lot of work into the staircase, even moving a carpet out of the way, but also for Niccolo's role, which now gets no kind of introduction. For ten seconds the camera is on the front door. Then the door opens, and Niccolo comes out, looks down the street for a split second, and then straightaway turns to look at the girl who's following him down the stairs. In no time she's passed him, and is walking down the street. Niccolo watches her go, then takes off after her. What worries me isn't just that our main view of Niccolo is from behind, but that, even more seriously, anyone seeing the film must surely conclude that he and the girl live in the same place and know each other. The script has him going into a strange house and looking inquisitively around the stairwell, when a girl comes down the stairs . . .

So both cameras are on the street. The second is moved several times, until finally it's at such an oblique angle that Niccolo doesn't even appear in shot until the girl is past him – when we get to see him from behind. I urge Michelangelo to try it with a camera inside, so that we can see Vincent from the front at least for a moment, but Michelangelo isn't moved. *Bene.* If we've learned anything in the past few weeks, it's that he knows his own mind.

The beginning of the story is, of course, strikingly similar to the beginning of the Portofino episode, where the man and the woman also met in a doorway. But the path there was so narrow that the shots had to be close-ups. Here, both cameras are wide. The second camera is now positioned in such a way that it's getting a parallel picture to the first, only not quite so wide, and then purely because we only have one zoom lens that opens to 20 mm. My aversion to the 'bi-cameral' method is given new fuel.

Then Jörg makes his first appearance on Steadycam, and, in spite of his beginner's nerves, he makes a brilliant job of it. He handles the equipment like a virtuoso, waltzing that heavy thing around and swinging it to and fro as though it weighed nothing at all. Because he makes it all look so much fun, he swiftly conquers the hearts of the all-Italian camera crew, who looked at him somewhat askance to begin with. Soon they're all watching him open-mouthed, like children.

I'm hugely relieved, because with Jörg we have a chance of really getting on top of this arduous shooting schedule, with all this long dialogue and walking scenes. For the most part, we won't have to bother about laying tracks: in Jörg we've found ourselves a one-man locomotive with built-in tracks!

After that, Michelangelo is too tired to continue. He's dropping off in front of the monitor, as he tends to do when he overtires himself. It took us far too long to get going today. Irene's make-up and costume were completely re-designed on location. It shouldn't happen like that.

So we take another look at the church, mainly to decide whether we ought to hire that expensive Zeppelin device or not. Michelangelo is simply unable to give us an answer on this point. With him, the scene has to be in hand before he's in any position to say what an adventurous bit of gadgetry like that would be able to contribute. Maybe the whole thing is a pipe dream of Enrica's. At any rate, it's not possible to get the equipment and the four men needed to run it up from Rome by Monday. And only if they were able to set up and rehearse on Monday would it be possible to fit those aerial shots in the church into our shooting plan. Otherwise, it would mean more departures from chronological order, and we've already found out how badly that throws us out. Finally, the decision has to be: Zeppelin, *nyet*. Stephane is mightily relieved that that little scheme's bitten the dust, especially when the monks let us know

Wenders confers with Vincent Perez

'He's tetchy, and loses his temper a couple of times': Enrica offers solace

The 'extremely friendly and chirpy' fathers of the parish of St Jean de Malte

at what times we need to break off our filming during our two days in their church so that they can celebrate Matins, Mass and Vespers.

I feel a bit wistful about the Zeppelin, because I'm convinced it could have been used to spectacular effect, especially in the awkward transition between Niccolo dropping off in the crowded church and waking up to find himself alone. Stephane comfortingly points out that I could always use the Zeppelin on my own shoot, where it would surely be easier to justify than getting it now for Michelangelo – who would need to have the thing demonstrated for him before he could even decide whether he wanted to use it or not.

There's something in what he says. Maybe when I get to write with Tonino, Aix will turn out to be one of my locations, too. And if so, then why not use the same church? It's quite possible that my framework and Michelangelo's episodes will end up having more to do with one another than we presently imagine.

I like our third couple very much indeed. Irene acts with warmth and conviction, with a great inner strength that one wouldn't at first expect in such a shy and delicate person. Vincent, by contrast, is more robust and confident, but without being at all overbearing. You might describe his attitude as a mixture of modesty and ambition. Irene is ambitious in her own way too, but she immerses herself in a thing so much that you aren't even aware of the ambition. In any case, the two of them are an extraordinary couple. It's easy to understand their fascination for one another. It's another casting triumph for Enrica and Michelangelo.

Michelangelo doesn't seem to be as elated as he was at the end of the Ferrara episode. He's tetchy, and loses his temper a couple of times. Also, his decisions aren't quite as impressive as on previous days, probably because he needs time to adjust to his new principals and to the new location.

A delightful surprise, though, are the extremely friendly and chirpy fathers of the parish of St Jean de Malte. They are a free community of eleven brothers, belonging to no order, but under the direct charge of the Bishop of Aix, who has entrusted them with this church and parish. A few of them are former Dominicans. As well as the care of souls, the monks have pledged themselves to research and study, and we're astounded to learn that some of them are experts on film, well acquainted with Michelangelo's work, and with mine too.

SATURDAY 3.12.94   Twenty-fourth day of shoot

We go back to filming in the streets of the old centre of Aix, carrying on where we left off yesterday: the walk and the dialogue of Niccolo and the girl. Michelangelo finally came up with a different set of locations – different parts of the same street, or facing a different direction – to the ones that had been prepared. That makes it all the more essential that we proceed in chronological order, and have a way out of each scene that gets us into the next one.

But for Jörg's feats with the Steadycam, we would have had another difficult day on set. The two actors are also outstanding, and know their lines inside out. Yesterday, Irene once said: 'Are you Protestant?' instead of 'Are you Christian?' and burst out laughing straight away at her own slip.

On the next location, I am surprised that Michelangelo wants to include the whole of a long and important piece of dialogue, when it had originally been intended that he would only shoot the first few sentences of it there. The scene begins with a reflection in a shop window, which looks terrific – a suggestion of Enrica's which Michelangelo took up. Then the actual protagonists come into shot, are picked up on the Steadycam, and carry on down the street until we can hardly hear them; even the monitor shows a blizzard, because the Steadycam's transmitter is out of range.

That mid-shot of our couple is followed by Michelangelo with two close-ups, again taken on the Steadycam, going backwards. We haven't done anything like that yet. The close-ups show what outstandingly professional actors we have.

We carry straight on through lunch, to keep the continuity of the light, till finally we break off for the day at half past three, ravenous, and go off to eat. Everyone is in a good mood. Today tested us to the limit, and the two new actors have given us a lot of fresh energy. After our late lunch it's too dark to carry on filming, so we suddenly find ourselves with time on our hands to explore the city.

Donata and I happen to notice a poster for a Salgado exhibition in the Cité du Livre, entitled 'La Main de l'Homme'. Today's the last day, and it's open for another hour. We ask passers-by for directions, and reach the exhibition at a jog.

We're bowled over by these wonderful photographs, every one of which is 'right' and convincing. All the photos show people working with their hands, and the subjects are from all five continents. Their quality is so sensational that we both feel inclined to view our own efforts as amateurish. They are so bold and unconditional in their pursuit of the reality they want to capture, so saturated in the worlds of the various sorts of work they explore that they seem to have a holy aura about them. They are as monumental as August Sander's 'People of the Century'.

SUNDAY 4.12.94   Twenty-fifth day of shoot

We carry on where we left off yesterday: at the fountain we were just approaching with the Steadycam. Irene and Vincent enter the shot, Niccolo hesitates, sees the fountain, and lets the girl walk on while he quickly has a drink. Then he runs and catches her up again. A pretty scene, really, but Beatrice, Aruna, Alfio and I are once more driven to despair: Michelangelo is intent on having them enter shot from the left. In aesthetic terms that's absolutely fine, and accords with the location and Michelangelo's sense of it. But yesterday's walk with the Steadycam was a brisk right-to-left movement across the screen, so that they have to appear from the right. If they come on from the left, there'll be an almighty 'crunch'. But Michelangelo, as ever, is indifferent to that, and all our pleading for 'proper continuity' leaves him cold.

Finally, though, once he's got his three takes in the bag, he allows us one alternative take our way, with the actors entering shot from the 'right' – and the right – side. Enrica announces the take with the words 'Wim will direct this one . . .' and I wish the earth would swallow me up. Of course I don't 'direct' it at all, I just get the same set-up and have the actors appearing from the right, whereupon Vincent stops and sees the fountain, and everything else is exactly as in the other shot.

Michelangelo makes it pretty clear that he doesn't think much of this version. Of course he'll cut it the way he wants, but, we console ourselves, his editor might be pleased if he can have the couple walking on in the same direction. We'll see . . .

We move punctually on to our next location – and everything grinds to a halt. At first it's the sun shining down into the narrow alleyway. The contrast is too much for our camera, so we decide to have lunch early. Lunch, yet again, isn't one hour but more like two, and once we're back in the alley, it's pitch dark.

Michelangelo sets up two cameras which keep getting in each other's way: one the Steadycam, the other on a tripod. Our couple is joined by a 'passer-by' with whom Niccolo has a brief exchange, and however we try and fiddle it, it seems impossible to get these three people equally well in shot for both cameras. Either they look good on the steady, or on the other, but not both. It's hopeless. Michelangelo is in a bad mood, and the camera crew are grumpy with the maestro.

And then the Steadycam keeps getting in the view of the fixed camera. If we'd filmed it as two separate shots, it would all have been done long ago, but this is just frustrating. When Michelangelo then has a forty-metre length of track laid down – which actually does nothing but replicate the path of the Steadycam anyway – the crew is almost mutinous and the light is gone. Certainly, there's no way we can claim any continuity with the two previous shots. The situation would have its blackly funny side, if it weren't for the fact that no one seems to be taking their

Setting up a serious length of track for a travelling shot

work seriously any more, partly because of that stupid length of track, which is serving no purpose whatsoever.

Then it's decided we're going to finish off the scene at the end of next week. Effectively we've achieved nothing today. The actress who plays the passer-by was flown up from Rome, and she's going to have to be brought in again next week, just for her little exclamation: 'Mais vous êtes fou!' It's all a bit extravagant. The mood is flat, the general disappointment all too palpable after yesterday's euphoria.

I've felt completely redundant all day, and can't work up much enthusiasm about anything. How could I? Michelangelo has me on as tight a rein as he has everyone else. Today he was as uncommunicative as it's possible to be. Yesterday at midnight he staged a bit of a protest in the hotel, and insisted that he wanted to look over all his night locations again right away. Then he went round them all, rejected them, and substituted others. The production department is in despair. They don't have permission to shoot in any of these new streets. And even if they had, no one has any idea how they are to be cleared of cars, barred to pedestrians and lit. When you factor in the artificial rain we want, the whole thing seems impossible. Beatrice's nerves are completely frazzled. After all, she's the one who's responsible for the schedule. She tries to remain calm about her lack of power. It's touching to see how, far from exploding with rage, she's thinking in her maternal way about how to make Michelangelo feel a bit better.

He is tired and irritated. Today everyone is made the object of his anger. He simply hasn't got this town and this episode under control yet, or that's how it appears.

In the evening, the French members of the crew give a party for their German and Italian colleagues. A jazz band led by Raphael, our trainee, plays brightly. There's dancing, and everyone perks up again. It seems this crew won't stay down for long: there is an essential friendliness in the people, and an incredibly generous insistence that this extraordinary film somehow gets made.

MONDAY 5.12.94   Rest day

In the morning we watch the rushes from the last couple of days in Ferrara. They are exceptionally good, among the best of the shoot so far. The closing shots of the Ferrara episode, in particular, are great cinema, and force Donata and me to reconsider our ideas for the framing story. We had thought of not having the 'director' figure at all.

Among my notes are such things as a science-fiction frame: these four lost episodes are discovered in a future time that has no cinema . . .

The actors, all forty years older, remember . . .

A detective story, instead of the 'director' . . . ?

But these rushes convince me that I have to keep the 'director' and shoot in Ferrara.

The 'Cézanne' cinema is showing *Paris, Texas*, the film I proposed for a discussion evening with the local film club. I haven't watched it with an audience since Cannes in 1984, and must admit I am very moved by it now. Michelangelo watches it with me, very alert, and stays for the whole discussion afterwards, along with the actors and most of the crew.

TUESDAY 6.12.94   Twenty-sixth day of shoot

And the first in the Church of St Jean de Malte. The monks are concentrating hard, rehearsing the choral piece they're going to sing for us, and impatient to make their screen debut, but unfortunately there's a little way to go until that happens. The church is the biggest set we've worked in so far, and it will take a while for Alfio and his crew to light it. After Michelangelo has confirmed that the first shot will be a big master of the church, we can go back to the hotel for a few hours. It gives us the opportunity to spend the rest of the morning with our visitors, the screenwriter Nicholas Klein and Bono from U2, and talk about our joint project, *The Million Dollar Hotel*.

Then in the afternoon, we film the first shot. Niccolo and the girl enter the church. She sits down in one of the front pews, while he carries on down the aisle and looks around. The choir is singing beautifully under the direction of Brother Daniel, and it's a promising opening for the scene.

We then start preparing the next shot. I'm a bit distracted, because in addition to Bono and Nicholas, there's someone here from the German television station WDR. When I return to the set, having been away for a while, I'm astonished to see they haven't got any further. The lights have been set up, but no one seems to know exactly what the shot is going to be. It's another one of those awful mix-ups, where everyone thinks Michelangelo has prescribed the route for the camera, when what he's drawn is the route for the actors. By the time I'm able to explain that the camera should be pointing the other way, it's too late to rearrange all the lighting for today.

Moreover, the monks celebrate Vespers at seven, so we need to be out of the church in any case. We leave our location feeling somewhat frustrated, once again having failed to achieve much, even though many of us have worked all day.

The monks have asked us – Irene too – to share their evening meal. It turns out that these monks are not mere cinephiles, they're veritable film-nuts. They've all seen Kieslowski's *Trois Couleurs: Rouge*; one of them even saw it three times in succession so he knows quite a few of Irene's lines off by heart. Their abbot knows all of Michelangelo's films, and says his favourite is *Identificazione di una donna*; another of them has come all the way from Switzerland for the shoot, and he's actually a film critic on the side.

So we spend a very pleasant evening together. Irene and I have questions hurled at us, and it could have gone on long into the night if Jean-Pierre Ruh hadn't arranged a sound-only date with the choir, to get a clean recording of their singing, without all the daytime din and the passing cars. And so the evening comes to a slightly abrupt end.

Certainly, none of us had imagined that a monastic community could be as jolly and open-minded as this one.

Two of the monks come over to the hotel after evensong, and I stay up talking to them till after midnight. They want to start a magazine called 'Pierre d'angle' or 'Cornerstone', and, depending on how much time I have to spare in the next few days, want to do a long interview with me for it.

WEDNESDAY 7.12.94 Twenty-seventh day of shoot

Alfio and his lighting crew have been working on the relighting of the nave since seven this morning, but even so, it isn't ready for us to shoot till after lunch. The next shot is extremely complicated, because almost the whole of the church is visible in it. Niccolo walks down the aisle as far as the altar. From there he looks briefly at the girl, and then he turns and strolls back. The camera is now looking the other way. He sits down in an empty pew, looks around a while, and finally goes to sleep. In the background you see the service going on, dominated by the choral singing.

I like the lighting, and Michelangelo's framing. There are a lot of takes. Then Michelangelo does a mid-shot of the girl, standing praying among the other worshippers. Alfio and I manage to persuade Michelangelo to use a second camera which shows Irene from a better angle – in a half-profile from in front. Michelangelo's mid-shot was from the side, and less pleasing. But both together come out speedily and very well, and suddenly we find ourselves facing the possibility that we might yet complete the shoot in the church today, and on schedule.

The last shot is another master, this time facing the door. Niccolo wakes up, finds himself in the empty church, and hurries to the exit. Again, Alfio and I inveigle a second camera into the proceedings at the last moment (I'm rapidly becoming a believer in two cameras!), to take a near shot of Niccolo, so that we have a bit more of him than just the huge master. Michelangelo shoots so sparingly, and every set-up takes such a long time, that a second camera can be really worth having, because it will allow him more flexibility to cut and edit.

Thanks to the patience of the friars, who agree to postpone their evening worship by half an hour, we really do finish the church scene as planned, six shots in all. Aruna timed the scene at between eight and nine minutes. I'm curious whether Michelangelo will leave it at that length when he edits.

Then we look at the rushes from the first two days in Aix. I have to say I think I was right about the opening shot. You simply don't realize when you see it that this is supposed to be the first meeting between two strangers. The rushes have come out rather blue, which makes Irene's make-up rather obtrusive – and she's supposed to have the natural look! The Steadycam shots look rather jittery. I'm very dissatisfied, and I'm angry with myself for not having intervened a little more decisively in one shot or the other.

The long walk that follows on from the reflection in the window seems to show nothing but walls plastered with graffiti – which we really didn't have to come to Aix-en-Provence for. That's also attributable to filming with two cameras, and the permanent compromises you have to strike when you do that. The Steadycam – because of the presence of the other camera – wasn't allowed to point back down the street, so you get both actors, walking at a fast pace, *in profile*, which is disturbing to look at and not particularly helpful for the dialogue. If we'd filmed with one camera at a time, we could have had the Steadycam going along *in front of* the actors, looking back down the street, instead of at all the graffiti to the side.

If only, if only . . . It's easy to be wise after the event, but when I spot my own mistakes afterwards, it's easier for me to cope with them than in my present situation, where I can see the 'mistakes' even while we're shooting but, like in some kind of nightmare, I'm unable to do anything to prevent them. Not that everything Michelangelo has shot in Aix is a nightmare – of course not, but at exactly the point where his infirmity tells, and at exactly the point where I should have intervened, I couldn't, because he wouldn't accept my help.

It's a shame that Jörg got such an unpromising assignment right at the beginning. The different picture sizes of the Steadycam don't fit together very well. In a word, I'm pretty downcast. While the last rushes were exhilarating, this set is a downer. Other people feel the same way, and they have mistakes of their own to chew over. Esther doesn't like Irene's coat or the colour of her dress, Judith is upset about the make-up being too obtrusive, Jörg finds his camerawork too restless. Alfio frowns, and Pino shrugs awkwardly. After the screening we all leave the cinema downcast, without speaking to one another.

Thursday 8.12.94   Twenty-eighth day of shoot

A day of crisis, at least for me. I don't seem to be able to do anything today. I feel more superfluous than ever, if not a downright irritant, and for a while I lapse into the same state of cynicism that quite a few of the crew have fallen into.

Donata gets me to snap out of it. We have a long talk, and I see everything slightly differently as a result. So what was it about?

Michelangelo had set up our last daylight shot (before our two protagonists enter the church) in such a way that, once again, the lens was full of disfigured walls, and all we saw of the beautiful Church of St Jean de Malte at the end of the Rue Cardinale was the façade up to its portals. The view down the street was also blocked off, so we really had to wonder why it needed to be barricaded off for the whole of the past week. We couldn't film before late afternoon, on account of the light, so we spent most of the day waiting to do one shot. The irritation from yesterday's rushes continues unabated. ('What are we doing filming in Aix if all you see of the city is walls covered with scribbles?')

Then the tracks are laid, but clearly not where they ought to be laid, because the fountain is in the way of the church door, and obscures the actors as they walk into the church. Michelangelo has this pointed out to him repeatedly, but today is one of those days when he dismisses any suggestion or objection out of hand. The dialogue begins to show certain discrepancies too. Irene says 'Let's hurry!', but at that very moment, Michelangelo wants them both to slow down ('Piano!'). Niccolo, who according to the screenplay is supposed to be the one who knows his way around the city, and knows a shortcut to the church, is asking the girl for directions – when, as she says in the very next sentence, she isn't from here and can't possibly know. Everything needs to be rewritten to fit our new situation and location, and I sit down and work it out with the actors. Michelangelo has no interest in these changes. When we rehearse the dialogue, he even makes a point of taking off his headphones.

When I go back to him after talking to the actors, he points at himself: 'Those are my actors, you keep away from them!' And when, in a situation of general confusion, I try to intervene, Michelangelo even grabs hold of my coat to stop me.

By the end of the day I've had enough, and I feel completely redundant. Michelangelo's efforts to cut me out are hurtful: he seems still, or perhaps once again, not to trust me; he won't believe I'm here to try and help, and persists in seeing me as his 'rival' or 'enemy'.

Alfio and I suggest a second camera, but he rejects that idea. Then Enrica manages to suggest a master in which there's at least a better view of the church. And that's it for the day. All we have to show for it are two basic shots that might have been done in an hour!

Donata points out that Michelangelo's displays of competitiveness tend to occur on days when he's evidently unsure of himself, and so they're perfectly understandable really; in his position, I would be just the same. Moreover, I'm not exactly enamoured of what's being filmed today, and Michelangelo must sense my reservations.

Why is it so hard to watch the filming in a neutral, unpartisan way? Why is it such a strain to follow a shoot which one can't influence, or at least not much? At the end of a day when we did two straightforward shots, I feel more knackered than if I'd filmed the most taxing scenes myself.

I feel this third episode is going badly wrong. The actors, good as they are, aren't able to show themselves, and their story leaves one cold. In the first two episodes, there was a tension right from the start. From the very first shot, a situation was created that gripped you and forced you to watch it unfold. Here in Aix, we've failed to generate this tension. Everything seems so rushed, I'm not even completely sure if the dialogue makes sense.

I hope to God I'll feel better in the morning. If not, maybe I should ask Michelangelo straight out whether he'd prefer it if I didn't appear on set. Maybe he would recover the authority he had at the end of the Ferrara episode if there wasn't somebody looking over his shoulder the whole time. Maybe he's worried that I'll disagree with him, or use my presence to bring his competence into question.

'Everything has got to change!' That's what Kamikaze scribbled on a piece of paper in *Kings of the Road*, in a situation when he was at his wits' end, much as I am now.

The film needs some backbone right now. That's what I am for the producers – their 'back-up man'. I've been that for the crew on many an occasion. But today it's the backbone that needs support. I'm not in this film for the sake of the producers. But what am I in it for, if Michelangelo sees me as a competitor?

FRIDAY 9.12.94   Twenty-ninth day of shoot

Went to work with fresh courage and goodwill. It's the first night shoot tonight. From now till the end of the shoot in Aix, we'll only be working at night.

The programme for the day – or should I say night – consists of two shots that ought to be reasonably straightforward, at least in terms of content: Niccolo comes out of the church and starts running down the street. Alfio and his team of electricians have been lighting the entire length of the Rue Cardinale since about ten this morning. Michelangelo showed us the two shots last night, and we're sticking to that. We add a second camera, and the first will shoot both set-ups with a variety of lenses. The night's work is over quite quickly.

Michelangelo and I are pals again. We happen to find ourselves standing side by side in the church, having gone in there to take shelter from the rain that has set in tonight – perfect timing for us, as it happens. We exchange brief looks, then nod and shrug our shoulders, and somehow, just like that, everything is all right between us once more.

The rushes are so-so. Only the scene with Veronica is downright annoying. It's not Jörg's Steadycam that's the problem, but the fixed camera, which is inexplicably badly framed, chopping off the actors' legs for no reason that I can see. It annoys me, because it's the fault of that mindless, slavish obedience again: Michelangelo wanted a fixed image and he set it up, without having followed the actors' movements through the camera, and good old Pino kept the same bottom frame, even though Vincent took a step backward, and thereby got his feet cut off in the picture. Really, the shot is unusable. The whole scene might just as well have been taken on the Steadycam.

Later we carry on looking for locations for next week's street scenes.

'Michelangelo and I are pals again . . .'

. . . even if the weather remains changeable.

Saturday 10.12.94 Thirtieth day of shoot

Today's programme is much more demanding than yesterday's: two pages of dialogue, when Niccolo catches up with the girl at the fountain, after the church.

During the run-through at noon, Michelangelo keeps his cards predictably close to his chest, and won't reveal how he intends to shoot the scene. 'Tutto!' he indicates, and gestures round the whole fountain. Alfio counters that it can't possibly be lit, and that he will have to make do with a 180-degree turn. Michelangelo wants to use the Steadycam. But that doesn't seem appropriate for a night scene with some rather crucial dialogue, plus the Steadycam casts rather unpredictable shadows. We persuade Michelangelo to come back at five o'clock to look at the lighting, and make his mind up then. He seems agreeable to that.

By six o'clock everything's ready, and we can rehearse again. Irene and Vincent are well prepared. Alfio has to talk Michelangelo into shooting a kind of master first of all, with one camera, and then, after a relight, taking some closer shots of the actors. Michelangelo needs some persuading that it's not possible to go in with three cameras, and shoot the master and a couple of close-ups simultaneously, in these night conditions. If he insisted on that, Alfio declares he would have to go on strike. The lighting would inevitably be such a botched job that he would refuse to have anything to do with it. His half-comic, half-melodramatic threat works. For the first time, we film in classical fashion: master, relight, close-up, relight, reverse angle.

And so everything takes a turn for the better. Irene and Vincent improve with every take, and the close-up of Irene is one of the best things we've done. There's a brief moment of panic when, following the second relighting, Michelangelo suddenly doesn't want to do the close-up of Vincent at all. He's satisfied that he's got a good close-up of his heroine. But he simply *has* to film a matching close-up of Vincent! The close-up of Irene is bound to contain fuzzy stretches or just a few less intense moments, simply because of the difficult lighting conditions if nothing else, and if he can't then cut to Vincent, he'll once again be tearing his hair out at the editing table. The only thing that cuts any ice with Michelangelo is the argument that Irene will also appear in the close-up of Vincent because of a slight change of position. That prompts him to go ahead with it. And that last shot is really the crowning moment of the whole scene; both actors are quite outstanding in it.

It's the first time we've filmed in a thoroughly conventional way with one camera at a time, relighting after each shot. By the time we've finished it's two a.m., but the whole crew are on a high because everyone senses that something important has been accomplished, and that the long hours of work have really borne fruit.

I collapse into bed, exhausted but happy. I think ten days of antibiotics have done their bit to weaken me too. (The doctor called again yesterday and listened to my lungs, but instead of taking me off the antibiotics, he actually doubled the dosage. I've still got quite a bad case of bronchitis, and I break out in a heavy sweat after any exertion.)

SUNDAY 11.12.94   Rest day

Donata and I have a lie-in. In the afternoon, we drive over to Cézanne's mountain, the Mont Sainte Victoire. It's a beautiful crisp winter's day. We don't exactly have the place to ourselves, so we just take a short walk and decide to come back during the week some time.

The evening sky is full of incredible colours, caused by a haze that hangs over the whole region. There must have been a big fire somewhere. It feels almost like a fairy-tale film, and we return to Aix completely astounded by the brilliant red, blue and green skies we're driving into. I only have my sunglasses, because I dropped my glasses in the shower this morning. I hope I can get replacement lenses here in Aix tomorrow, otherwise I won't be much use on the next night shoot.

In the evening, Donata drives to Nîmes. I go to evening Mass at St Jean de Malte, stay on for Vespers, and afterwards walk the streets for a couple of hours, thinking about my frame narrative.

My favourite idea at the moment is that Michelangelo's episodes could be seen to emerge from a reading of his book *Quel bowling sul Tevere*. All it would take is a storyteller and/or a reader. Marcello Mastroianni perhaps? This notion is largely influenced by the fact that for the past fortnight I've been reading Peter Handke's new novel *My Year in No Man's Bay*, which has been making me think of the idea of the storyteller. Or a cinema narrator, perhaps? But that way lies *Cinema Paradiso*.

My own preference would be for a frame with some humour in it. But that would run the risk of being too wrapped up in itself, and it would probably hurt Michelangelo's episodes if they were surrounded by laughter.

More tomorrow.

MONDAY 12.12.94   Thirty-first day of shoot

When we meet Michelangelo on the terrace at noon, we get a sense right away that today isn't going to be easy. The sun is shining and the air is clear, but he looks grumpy. He seems impatient. Something is amiss, but he can't or won't tell us what it is.

I order some new glasses, which are ready two hours later. Now I can at least follow the night shoot without blundering around in the dark in my sunglasses.

By the time we start rehearsing at six Alfio has lit the way through three streets, and, as he understood Michelangelo's request, laid some tracks. But everything turns out differently. Michelangelo does indeed stage the encounter between Niccolo and the girl and a band of youths in the first street, but a long way down it, so that Alfio is forced to relight everything. Then, our two leads take up different positions from those they took up during the rehearsals, so the lighting has to be altered a second time. I'm amazed at Alfio's patience with all these changes.

Any comments and questions get jumped on by Michelangelo

today. 'Zitto!' he keeps saying, 'Shut up!', and Enrica fares worst of all. Finally, she loses her nerve, and stops trying to find out what he wants. He then directs the scene in such a way that the lines make no sense at all. In the screenplay, Niccolo gallantly 'protects' the girl against the onrushing horde, but today Michelangelo doesn't want that. Niccolo isn't even to lay a finger on her. Her protest, in the script, that he shouldn't treat her like a woman, thereby loses its point. But no one can change Michelangelo's mind today, not even Alfio, who's trying to stick up for his lighting. He's cleverly put up a spotlight on the opposite side of the street. But no, that's where Michelangelo now wants the scene to take place, and the two principals are to carry on walking too. On the other side of the street, without the spotlight, the scene looks flat, and the dialogue makes no sense. But that's how we shoot it. 'Basta!' There's no discussion today.

For all my disagreement with Michelangelo in the course of the past few days, over his remote and chilly behaviour with all of us, I can somehow empathize with what he's doing. He needs to find his own way through the scene and disregard all the foolish or sensible suggestions he receives on all sides – my own included. He doesn't know the town well; at night and in Alfio's lighting it doesn't look the way it did in the recces. On top of that he can't really judge the French dialogue – all he has to go on is his instinct and his sense of form. And then in these circumstances to have another director alongside him, who is able to walk and talk, and talk in French at that . . . I can only guess how hurt, threatened, angry, provoked and hemmed in *I* would feel if it was me. When it comes down to it, Michelangelo has actually responded to my presence with an astonishing degree of calm. But is that really a more positive perspective on things than the ironic view I held before? 'We need to get through,' I muse, 'through this night-shoot, and through these obstacles.'

We continue after supper, with enormous difficulty: three further alleyways now come into shot, all linked up with a complicated track. It takes Alfio hours to light it, and by the time we're ready to rehearse it's well after midnight. The rehearsals go on for a long time, with technical difficulties largely to blame: Michelangelo wants to shoot the entire walk with the extended zoom, i.e. with a focal width of barely 100 mm. With the widest aperture, that means there is a margin of error of less than 5 cm with the focus. Which means the two actors will never be in focus at the same time. The camera has to rehearse it over and over again, mainly because their two heads are still not close enough for Michelangelo's liking, and he wants the actors to be even nearer to the camera. Alfio is miserable: he's done a beautiful job of lighting the three alleyways, and now you can hardly see any of it. Pino and his focus puller Mauricio are close to despair: in bright sunshine, and with an aperture of 11 or 16, the maestro had wanted to film nothing but long shots, no close-ups at all, and now, with an open aperture, he wants to go right in close. But that's the way he is: once he sets his heart on something, you can't hope to persuade him otherwise. But you can't miss the pride and admiration in their voices when the crew members say that.

And because all of us finally understand that, we do our best to see that all that effort so late at night pays off, and the scene does come out nicely, with its own curious intensity. There are still some difficulties – Vincent isn't as rock-solid with his lines as Irene is. Once, Michelangelo called 'Cut!' because Vincent hesitated over what he was saying. A pity, because I think his hesitation worked in the French: it didn't seem as though he'd dried up, rather that the character was looking for words. Michelangelo wants him more fluent, which, given the literary quality of the dialogue, means that Vincent is often declaiming or reciting rather than speaking. But in that moment, something was snapped off that might have given the scene greater credibility and human intimacy.

I try to help the actors with their lines. We sort out a few oddities of style, and keep going through the dialogue together. I try to do it unobtrusively so that Michelangelo doesn't notice. I know I'm not really going behind his back – quite the contrary.

But to persuade him of that once more is more than I can manage just now. So I do my work clandestinely. It's a pleasure to watch Irene and Vincent working together. They keep trying new things, repeat the text, improvise and suggest, without being too deadly serious about it.

At four in the morning we're finally finished, exhausted but happy. Right at the end, Michelangelo agrees that we can do one take with a shallower focus, with more of the location visible in the background. Alfio is beaming, because all his work will finally show, and even Michelangelo will be happy to have an alternative when he's editing.

Tuesday 13.12.94 Thirty-second day of shoot

Night again, in the Place d'Albertas. Consternation among the producers: Michelangelo is suddenly unhappy with the location! He's not happy with the transition from yesterday's scene. He's right too: from the narrow lane to the wide open square does seem a bit of a jump. We ought really to try and insert a further, intermediate location. We find one that he likes, right next to tomorrow's location, and we'll film a little bridging scene there.

After all the toing and froing, we end up filming in the Place d'Albertas after all. It's difficult to light, and again takes Alfio quite some time. Then, after a long and beautiful shot round the fountain, just as we're thinking that's it for the day, Michelangelo wants to do the whole thing again, only closer. No one expected that. For this version, filmed, once again, with extended zoom at maximum focal length, he changes the positions of the actors, bringing them closer to the camera, because with the 100 mm lens their faces aren't near enough for him. In other words, we need to relight. We can forget about going to bed anytime soon.

It's three in the morning when the last clapboard falls, and I snap some stills immediately afterwards, as usual. Everyone's pleased with the scene. The only question is whether the closer footage can be cut in or not.

WEDNESDAY 14.12.94 Thirty-third day of shoot

Night-shoot in the rain, continuing where we left off yesterday. Since we've been in Aix, all our filming has been in chronological order. A street is lit, the rain-machine set up. The two actors appear in the distance, and walk towards the camera. The rain gets heavier, and they start running, to seek shelter in a little passageway. The young woman stumbles and falls, but she's not hurt and bursts out laughing. Irene is brilliant; each time she falls headlong on the cobbles, quite alarmingly. As Donata says, she's a born actress, whose work is so natural and fearless and unobtrusive and precise that she makes it all look simple and utterly convincing. Even when something is difficult or unpleasant, like falling down in the rain, she makes it look as if it's the easiest thing in the world.

Following on from the establishing shot that shows the couple taking shelter from the downpour, Michelangelo wants to take a shot from inside the passageway. Alfio lights it, tracks are laid, but when Michelangelo comes and surveys everything, the tracks are taken up again. 'Via!' He won't even look at the shot that Alfio proposes. No – the countershot to the previous master has to be another master. But we all believe that the two sentences exchanged by the actors at this point are the most crucial of their whole nocturnal dialogue. Niccolo says: 'And what if I were to fall in love with you?' and she replies: 'That would be like lighting a candle in a brilliantly illuminated room . . .' So shouldn't we be a bit closer to them for that? No, Michelangelo doesn't want that at all. In the last couple of days, in most unfavourable conditions, he couldn't get close enough, whereas now, when he could shoot close-ups in good light, he wants to stay out.

Alfio has no idea how he's going to light this shot. The problem isn't the passageway itself, but the courtyard it leads into, which of course has to have rain falling in it too. But we haven't got permission to shoot there. Alfio's problem is that the rain needs to be backlit to make it visible to the camera. And that back-lighting can only be done from one of the balconies overlooking the courtyard – but of course we're not allowed to go up there. Anyway, it's the middle of the night, and the residents are asleep.

Time passes. No one knows how we're going to solve this problem, and we stand around for hours, not doing anything. Should we call it off, and come back tomorrow? Finally, the special effects crew manage to drape the rain-sprinkler nearer to the camera, and the lighting crew clamber up between the walls and hang up a light. It's worth the trouble; it's a beautiful shot, and by four o'clock we've done our bit for the day (or the night). The actors are both soaked, and everyone's exhausted.

Michelangelo's changed his mind about the extra shot he wanted yesterday. He decided it wasn't absolutely essential.

THURSDAY 15.12.94   Thirty-fourth day of shoot

For Donata and me, this is the last day of the first part of the shoot. Tomorrow we're flying off to Lisbon for the premiere of *Lisbon Story*.

We film the continuation of yesterday's rain scene. Niccolo and the young woman carry on walking through the rain, and reach the house where the episode began two weeks ago. They glance at each other, and then Irene vanishes into the house. Vincent stays in the rain for a moment, then rushes in after her. By the time we arrive, at seven o'clock, the scene has already been lit, and we're done by half past eight. And that's all for today.

It's suggested to Michelangelo that he might therefore start on tomorrow's staircase scene, and perhaps do the first shot now, and he agrees. It's our way of trying to find out what he has in mind for the scene. We've gone and looked at the stairs with him a couple of times in the last few days, trying to discover just that, but we weren't successful on either occasion. Alfio has stated quite categorically that he couldn't light the whole staircase in case Michelangelo – as he'd hinted previously – proposed to use the Steadycam, and cover all three floors in a single shot. He's worried that the narrow staircase hasn't anywhere where

A meaningful glance between Irene Jacob and Vincent Perez

he can hide his lights, so the Steadycam would have to keep going through a patchwork of light and its own shadow.

There's an impasse: Alfio won't light, and Michelangelo doesn't know how to shoot if he can't use the Steadycam. With Jörg we do a demonstration of two ways that the Steadycam might be used, without pursuing the actors up the stairs. Basically, in the first, the camera can watch the actors from below; in the second, from above. Michelangelo takes to the suggestion. Huge relief, especially for the producers. It's the first time in ages that Michelangelo has been willing to consider a suggestion, never mind accept it. Suddenly we've broken through. Alfio can go ahead and light, and Michelangelo knows how he's going to shoot, and can work on the idea.

It takes another couple of hours before we're finally ready, but then several wonderful shots of the staircase scene are filmed, some on Steadycam and a few on the dolly, by way of an alternative. It's just as well for Michelangelo to have so many alternatives, because it's by no means clear how he intends to cut, or indeed whether the dolly-shot will fit in with the Steadycam footage. It's therefore advisable to shoot from above and below, and to use them both.

The actors, both of whom have to stand outside the door in the pouring rain at the beginning of every take, end up soaked to the skin, and by the time we finish at four a.m. they're both sneezing.

Donata and I distribute farewell and Christmas gifts to the crew: books, and some pictures of the shoot, which Donata has spent the last few days choosing, framing and wrapping up, with help from Jolanda. It's a shame to have to leave a day before the end of the shoot, and we both feel as though we're deserting. But we couldn't put off Lisbon any longer. Tomorrow's date for the premiere was fixed a long time ago – before we even began filming with Michelangelo – and if we hadn't run up three extra days in Comacchio, we would have been finished the day before yesterday.

We sit up late with Vincent and Irene, drinking grogs in the bar. They were both really terrific, and we've become fond of them. It would be great if they were available to take part in my framework too.

Friday 16.12.94   Thirty-fifth day of shoot

We pack our bags in a rush the next morning. Jolanda is heading back to Berlin with all our things from the shoot, while we set off for Lisbon with just overnight bags. We have breakfast with Stephane in his house near Aix, and then off to the airport in Marseilles.

We arrive in Lisbon in the early evening.

The premiere is a catastrophe. The film has to be shown with a scratch mix in mono, because the stereo mix isn't going to be done till next month. My editor, Peter Przygodda, had five days in which to put it together. This screening is really a preview in all but name, and we will use it as a learning experience when it comes to the final edit.

But in its present form, I really can't relate to the film at all. It strikes me as jerky, unconsidered, rough. Donata and I wish the ground would open and swallow us up. Jürgen Knieper's music is generally too loud, and is cued in suddenly and often at the wrong moments, flattening everything else. The narrative dubs seem stuck on, the scenes themselves are too talky, and the whole thing has no flow.

There's no sign of Peter Przygodda afterwards. I'm really worried for him. Donata and I are completely shattered, and it's a real effort to get through the rest of the evening.

At half past three in the morning we call the production department in Aix, to find out how the shoot ended there. Perfect timing: they've just finished. Three complicated shots were done, and that's the end of the first part of the shoot. Michelangelo sounds relaxed and is laughing on the phone, Vincent and Irene are happy, Enrica, Beatrice and Andrea relieved. All *paletti*, and for a while we share their feelings and forget about the débâcle of *Lisbon Story*.

In the end, it's not going to be that bad. It just means there's work to be done – which we knew really, and would have done already if we hadn't had to come off the film a couple of months early.

There's a press conference tomorrow. We just need to get through that, and then we'll have a few days of badly needed rest.

Sunday 19.2.95

More than two months later, in Paris. We begin again tomorrow – rather later than originally planned – on Michelangelo's fourth and last episode. But in the meantime, 'Due telefaxi' has turned into 'Non mi cercare'.

A lot has happened since December. I took up *Lisbon Story* again, mixed it, and cut it by about ten minutes. It's now finished, and I'm thinking of showing it out of competition at Cannes, in the category called 'Un certain regard', which seems right for this little film.

Michelangelo's screenplay has been radically changed, because after a certain amount of toing and froing it proved impossible to realize 'Due telefaxi'. Everyone agreed that the twin skyscrapers of the Société Générale insurance company were the ideal place to shoot it, and Michelangelo was completely banking on its availability as a location. But a hold-up in the building work gave rise to a contractual stand-off between the builders and the architect, and the completion and handing over to the tenant couldn't be delayed any further by giving us the use of the building for a couple of weeks. We could, perhaps, have used it some time in April or May, but that would have been too late for our purposes anyway. A delay of that order was just unsustainable. Every week we don't shoot costs us money, eating into the budget that was left for Michelangelo's fourth episode and my frame story. So Michelangelo had to bite the bullet, and decide whether to look for another location for 'Due telefaxi', or else choose a different plot for his final episode. He went for the story option. Enrica, Tonino and I suggested he keep it in Paris. After re-reading *Quel bowling sul Tevere*, we came up with a new screenplay by amalgamating two of the stories, 'La rota' and 'Non mi cercare'. Initially Michelangelo rejected Tonino's suggestion, then he softened, and finally came round to it. Fanny Ardant remained the female lead, but our delay meant that Jeremy Irons, whom Michelangelo had wanted to play opposite her, was no longer available.

Michelangelo selected Jean Reno in his place. As the new story is about a triangular relationship, there was another couple to cast, and Michelangelo and Enrica went for Chiara Caselli and Peter Weller.

In January I got together with Tonino Guerra in Ferrara to work on the new episode and my framework. We decided not to tell the story in a series of flashbacks, the way it is in the book, but to proceed chronologically, which would certainly be helpful to Michelangelo when he came to direct it. It's a simple enough story. Roberto, an American who lives in Paris, meets an Italian woman, Olga, in a café, and she tells him a story. He falls in love with her. Later on: Roberto's wife Patrizia has been living with the knowledge that for the last couple of years her husband has had a lover. She can't stand it any more, and insists that he leave Olga. Roberto is unable to do so; in fact he is growing ever more dependent on her. But he promises Patrizia that he will break with Olga that very day. He sleeps with Patrizia for the first time in a long time. Olga feels betrayed by Roberto. They have an argument, which, however, ends up with them both in bed together. Roberto can't decide what to do . . . Carlo, a businessman, returns to his apartment after an extended absence, only to find it empty. His wife has left him, and taken all the furniture. Patrizia rings the doorbell. She has seen an ad that says the apartment is for rent. She's left Roberto, and wants to live on her own. Her furniture is already on its way. Carlo and Patrizia realize that they are in similar situations . . .

We devised and wrote my framework from scratch. We returned to the original concept of a 'director', but with a much clearer sense of it as a *diario mentale*, to use Tonino's phrase. It wasn't possible to write it all out, because Michelangelo first had to finish shooting, and we also needed to know the running order of the four episodes. For my own inserts, obviously, an awful lot depends on that.

The day before yesterday we saw Michelangelo's rough-cut, and were deeply impressed. Much of it moved me, especially the Aix episode. And I was particularly relieved to find that Ines and Kim were not disgraced; quite the opposite, they kept their end up admirably. Much was still too long, but one had a good sense of Michelangelo everywhere in it. These three episodes were his work, there was no mistaking that, and curiously enough they reminded me more of his early films than of his later work.

The Portofino episode seemed to be the most powerful of the stories, probably because it began so abruptly and directly, and continued so unhesitatingly. Much of that was thanks to John and Sophie.

All the actors seemed to give a good account of themselves. If the tempo were just tightened up a little bit the film would still keep its cool rhythm, and probably still seem 'long' without being boring.

Michelangelo himself was very pleased. I looked across at him in the dark from time to time, and saw tears in his eyes. Seeing him sitting there, upright and alert, clearly relating to the images on the screen, I was reminded once more of his dictum: 'Living, for me, means filming.' I always thought that was probably true for a lot of directors, but in the course of our time together I've seen how deeply it applies to Michelangelo, and what an existential experience filming is for him. Under his eye, every gesture and every camera movement becomes something necessary, immutable and unmistakable. At a time when so much that's shown in the cinema is random and interchangeable, he really is a monument to another ethos of image-making entirely.

There's one scene that's missing from the rough-cut: the dialogue under the arcades in Comacchio. Michelangelo hasn't included any of the footage that was taken, and terrifies the producers by declaring that he needs another four days to complete the episode. I'm sure that won't be possible. But maybe it's a way of trying to put off the inevitable end. It must be agonizing for Michelangelo to think that these are his last days behind a camera.

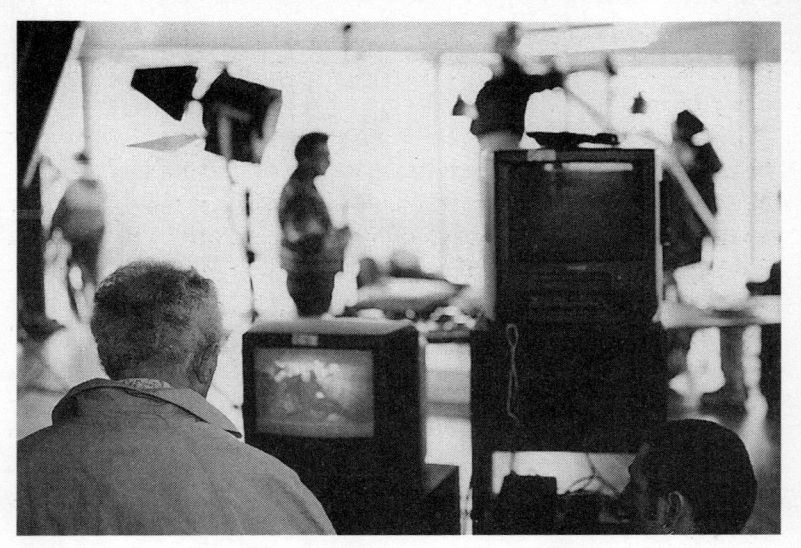

Setting up the Parisian apartment; the maestro at the monitor

Monday 20.2.95   Thirty-sixth day of shoot

A new location: an empty modern apartment high above the roofs of Paris, and it takes a long time for Alfio to light it. It's the penthouse of the Fondation Cartier. I'm partly responsible for its choice, since it was while I was talking to Jean Nouvel, the architect of this beautiful building, that I thought of showing it to Michelangelo. Thierry has done wonders, once again, and has dispelled the cool office ambience it formerly had. His decor makes it look like an ultra-modern apartment. I'd actually stopped proposing that we film here, because I thought it might pull against the story. But I was probably wrong: it looks quite spectacular, even though its glass walls make lighting it a nightmarish proposition. They reflect simply everything.

I spend most of the day hunched over my computer, rewriting my script – after seeing the rough-cut yesterday, I felt I simply had to. My part has to be calm and tranquil. While our two strands can perfectly well be distinct, I don't want to be working *against* Michelangelo's episodes.

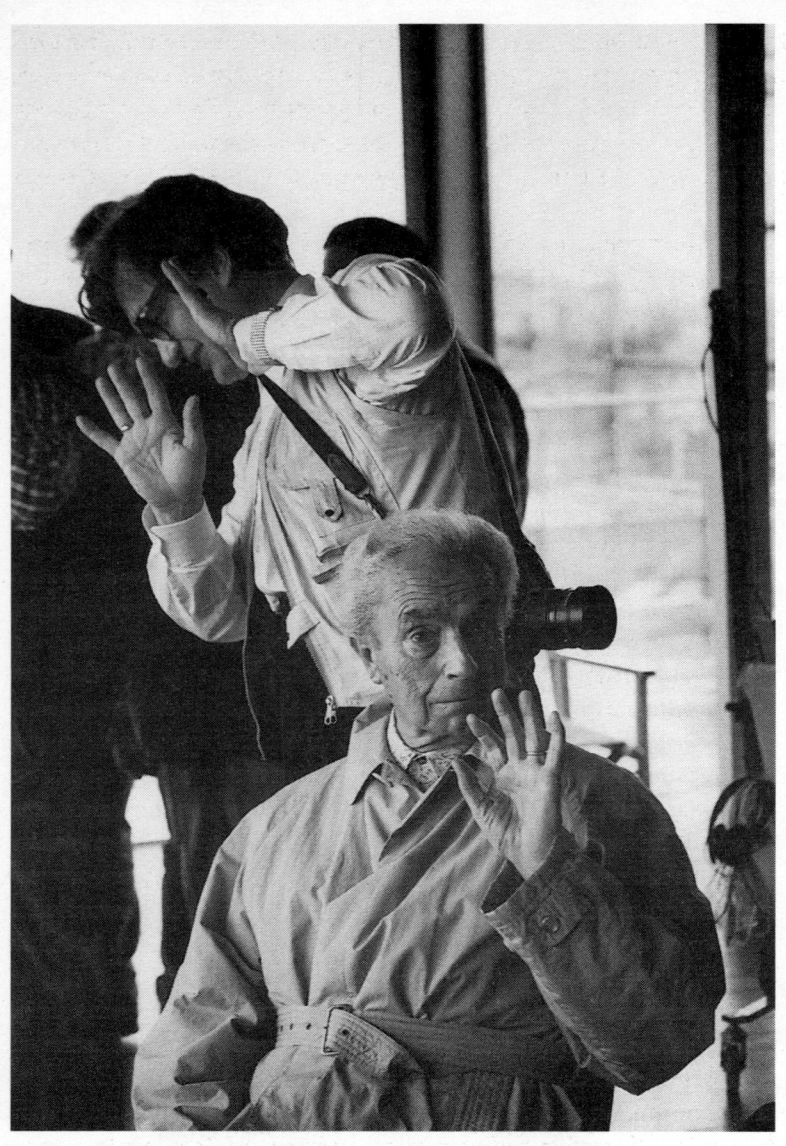

'Michelangelo is in terrific form today': the collaborators in self-mocking mode

The question of casting also raises its head. It no longer seems appropriate, as previously envisaged, to lift Michelangelo's actors from earlier or later episodes, and, as it were, 'recycle' them. On the contrary: I feel fairly sure they should be reserved for Michelangelo and his stories. Otherwise, I should be detracting from them.

The first scene of any length in my introduction, as presently envisaged by Tonino and me, is set in a museum in Ferrara, the famous Palazzo Schifanoia. The 'director', having just flown in, finds himself in the museum, and listens to a schoolteacher attempting to explain the murals to his class. Two of the figures in the fresco come to life in the eyes of the children. They are two lovers, of whom the teacher explains that they were made for each other, but could never meet. That states Michelangelo's theme of 'impossible love', and my plan is to cast Irene Jacob and Vincent Perez – the couple in Michelangelo's last episode – as the pair. That would create a bridge from the beginning of the film to the end.

Finally, after a few hours, we start shooting again. Michelangelo is in terrific form today. He seems completely transformed: cool, confident, in control. He's filming differently too: each shot leads to a point where he is certain he will cut, and at that point he stops and sets up the next scene. And so it goes, step by step. There is far more *découpage* than in the previous episodes, and the individual shots are much shorter. As ever, though, Alfio has no idea what will come next.

Today we're only filming with the one actor, Jean Reno, who strikes me as a rather atypical figure in an Antonioni film. He's a bit of a wild man, with pronounced comic leanings. But the two of them are working together very seriously; in fact, Michelangelo gives him more screen-time and more shots than any of his previous male leads. We're shooting the sequence where we first meet his character, Carlo, as he returns to his apartment, only to find it empty. After a while his wife phones him. Carlo demands an explanation, but she merely replies that he has left her once too often. 'Don't look for me!' she says before she hangs up. Hence the title of the episode.

Jean Reno: 'a bit of a wild man, with pronounced comic leanings'

I only go up on set when the shot has been planned and is being rehearsed. That way, I get a keen sense of the 'building block' style: one stone stood next to another. All perfectly chronological.

I carry on shooting my stills. It's fun taking pictures here. There's Paris on all sides, and the building itself is wonderfully photogenic.

TUESDAY 21.2.95   Thirty-seventh day of shoot

I'm still busy with my screenplay, and don't spend much time on set. I need to be finished by tonight, so that Beatrice can work out the shooting schedule and settle the budget. There are a load of small parts to cast, and a great many changes of scene. The script is therefore probably too long, maybe thirty minutes or more, instead of the twenty it's supposed to be. I wonder if it'll be possible to shoot it in a fortnight.

Michelangelo carries on filming exactly as he began yesterday. He takes amazing quantities of shots, and not one plan sequence among them. The day isn't easy, particularly for Alfio. The

Enter Fanny Ardant

weather is very changeable, so he has to keep altering the lighting because of all the glass walls.

Jean Reno is very funny. During takes he's always properly serious, but between takes it's impossible not to laugh at him and with him. He's up for any kind of joke or prank. What I particularly like about him is the way he treats everyone equally, whether they're trainees, sparks, fellow actors or producers.

It's the first day for Fanny Ardant, who plays Patrizia, but all we do with her today is the very first establishing shot of her entering the apartment, and Carlo explaining to her that it isn't for rent. The ad in the paper, which she holds under his nose, was a little private vendetta on the part of his wife. That's about all we're able to do with Fanny: she has a theatre engagement in the evening, and needs to leave punctually. That first shot wasn't even a proper warm-up for her.

By seven p.m. the first draft of my script is finished, and it fills twenty-two pages. Can that be squeezed into twenty minutes? Some of the sequences and a few of the images in it please me, but the rest is pretty uninspired. I read it aloud to Donata.

That's the acid test, and she duly points out all its weak points. I've still got a lot of work to do on it . . .

For that reason, we don't go to the rushes tonight. Later on, Enrica tells us on the phone that unfortunately yesterday's scenes came out awful. Maybe that's all down to the grading. Alfio had adjusted everything to the light outside, turning Jean Reno into a silhouette, whereas the copier had evidently gone by flesh-tones instead, which made the outside world look much too bright. I can imagine Michelangelo's reaction only too well. I hope a new set of rushes will show everything – literally – in a better light. At any rate, we decide to look at the adjusted rushes tomorrow before we start shooting, so that, if need be, we can re-shoot the beginning.

WEDNESDAY 22.2.95   Thirty-eighth day of shoot

Fanny's first 'proper' day of filming. Patrizia tells Carlo the sad story of her husband and his lover, whom he is unable to leave, even after repeated demands and ultimatums. To begin with Fanny has a touch of stage fright, but she gets her confidence back quickly. She and Jean make a curious couple, but they may be all the more believable for that.

She is a completely different type of actress to Ines, Sophie or Irene. There is really no such thing as a 'type of actor' anyway. Or, conversely, there are as many types as there are individual actors and actresses. Every actor represents his own school and style and method.

Michelangelo and Fanny hit it off right away, communicating with gestures and expressions. I seriously wonder whether Michelangelo would communicate any better if he could speak. The silent play of facial expressions and gestures he puts on with his female leads seems to me to 'speak volumes'.

Yesterday was overcast and showery. Because the sun is beating down today – which means that there is no continuity in terms of light – Michelangelo shoots everything towards the interior of the apartment, so that the windows are kept out of shot. I'm surprised, and find it remarkable – after some of our previous experiences – that he should be this flexible.

Michelangelo really doesn't need me at all. With some help from Beatrice, he's in complete command of his set. So I carry on working on my script, and turn up only for the actual filming and the stills afterwards.

Michelangelo is still filming shot for shot with great certainty and authority, but still without ever letting anyone know where the camera is going to be for the next set-up. His directing continues to be more detailed than in the earlier episodes. Every shot seems just right. He's really flowing now, and gives off a wonderful calm.

The location is looking better and better, and any worries of mine that it might somehow work against the story appear to be quite groundless.

In the evening, Donata and I are asked to dinner by Marcello Mastroianni. Marcello is impatient to get his hands on the script. But for the time being, all I can do is tell him about it.

THURSDAY 23.2.95   Thirty-ninth day of shoot

We are filming the ending of the encounter between Patrizia and Carlo. He kisses her hand in farewell, and she strokes his face. The effect of the scene is a little elegiac, but it's carried by the believability of the two principals. Michelangelo is still in great form; if anything, he's enjoying himself even more than on previous days.

Fanny will go on filming next week: she has her scenes with her 'husband', Roberto, played by Peter Weller. Jean Reno has one more day, tomorrow, on his own.

I spend a lot of time at the computer, shortening my screenplay. A few of the cuts are easy to make, others less so. I can't commit myself to any final order, because there's still some uncertainty whether Michelangelo is going to stick to the Ferrara/Portofino/

Paris/Aix order, or move Paris to the end. That would really throw my screenplay off balance.

In the afternoon I call on Jeanne Moreau, who has agreed to appear in a scene with Marcello! I'm delighted about that. Working with Jeanne on *To the End of the World* ranks among my best experiences.

FRIDAY 24.2.95   Fortieth day of shoot

So today we shoot with Jean Reno on his own: first of all his arrival in the building, then a scene in the lift. The pretty straightforward external shot takes us all morning. Everyone is distracted and uncoordinated, and Michelangelo seems to be in bad shape as well. He's caught a chill and sounds hoarse.

It's worse after lunch. He has a bad cough, and probably a slight temperature. He decides to go and lie down in his room, and asks me to take over for the last shot. We discuss it briefly and then, for the first, and I hope only, time, I take over as his back-up.

We shoot Jean's lift scene on the Steadycam, and without a cut. Jean enters the building, crosses the lobby, holds the lift open for a woman who comes running to catch it, and then goes up to the penthouse floor with her. Down in the lobby, the camera retreats in front of Jean, enters a second lift, films Jean and his companion through the glass walls, gets out at the top and observes the woman unlocking the apartment. It's quite a complicated shot, not least in terms of the perpetually changing qualities of the light, and we also have a hard time synchronizing the two lifts. We don't seem to be able to dispatch them at the same time; either the one with the camera goes off by itself, or the one with the actors. It's maddening. Then the daylight starts to go, and I'm not able to offer Michelangelo the one perfect take I would have loved to have for him.

It's quite a strain, going from my desk to the set, and by evening I'm exhausted, in large part because my little shoot didn't pass off as immaculately as I had hoped. Jörg on the

Steadycam did his best, and Alfio was able to keep adjusting the lighting too, but the darned lifts wouldn't co-operate. However, there's nothing I can do about it now.

In the evening there are some costume trials for Chiara Caselli, who plays the young woman who wrecks Patrizia and Roberto's marriage.

Saturday 25.2.95   Forty-first day of shoot

Really just a half-day. The crew is getting the afternoon off. Michelangelo isn't properly fit yet, so we just film one shot: a master of the Paris bistro where Olga speaks to Roberto (Peter Weller) for the first time.

I work on the dialogue with the two actors, trying to make it a little more fluent and speakable. Peter's French is very good for an American, and Chiara's Italian accent isn't too obtrusive either.

Italian TV is taking a few shots of the set. Alfio is once more in despair, because the location, the brasserie of the Hotel Lutetia, is walled with mirrors, so it's practically impossible to light.

Half a day in a Parisian bistro: Antonioni with Peter Weller

It's the evening that the French film prizes, the Césars, are awarded. I was talked into presenting the award for the best foreign film, along with Costa-Gavras. To our great surprise, we don't hand the massive statue to Steven Spielberg for *Schindler's List*, but to Mike Newell for *Four Weddings and a Funeral.* We really hadn't planned on that at all; everyone reckoned Spielberg was a certainty. I would have liked to give it to him too, as he had just said a few wonderful words of support for European film, and the fight to maintain the identity of European cinema.

At the ceremony we meet up with Irene Jacob again, who's looking forward as much as we are to our shoot in Ferrara in a couple of weeks.

SUNDAY 26.2.95   Rest day

A rest day, but not for us. In the morning we work on the shooting schedule with Beatrice, and at midday we fly to Milan. *Lisbon Story* is being released in Italy this week. There are a couple of interviews in the afternoon and dinner with the distributor and some people from the Triennale, who've set up the events for tomorrow. It was all planned a long time ago, when it seemed completely unimaginable that we'd still be filming in February.

MONDAY 27.2.95   Forty-second day of shoot

But not for Donata and me, still in Milan. I'm busy giving interviews on *Lisbon Story* all day, in the afternoon there's a panel discussion with some architects, and in the evening a benefit screening for the FAI, an Italian body that's responsible for looking after historical monuments.

Beatrice assures us on the telephone that everything's going smoothly back in Paris. Michelangelo was feeling better, and completed the day's schedule on time: the long dialogue scene in the bistro with Peter Weller and Chiara Caselli, doing the text we had previously worked on with them. There had even been a few close-ups, very large ones at that, using a 250 mm lens. I would like to have been there for that. Michelangelo never ceases to amaze me. Even his long shots, in their way, are as extreme as his close-ups.

At night, we take the sleeper back; it's the only way we'll be back on set in good time tomorrow morning.

TUESDAY 28.2.95   Forty-third day of shoot

From the station to the hotel, showered, changed, and then out to location, a house in Sceaux, a southern suburb of Paris. In the story, that's where Patrizia and Roberto live. In the first scene she's sitting in a dark corner in the small hours, waiting for her husband to come home. Then she causes a jealous scene, accusing him of having been with his girlfriend again. It emerges from the dialogue that his extra-marital relationship has been going on for three years already.

For the first time in several days, Michelangelo wants to shoot with two cameras again. Alfio has difficulty lighting, and he can't light Fanny as he would like. But, as one might expect, Michelangelo doesn't care about that.

I've kept out of things for a long time now, but today I roll up my sleeves a bit and work with the actors to improve their French texts. Peter Weller, in particular, is terribly scrupulous and concerned about every line, every word. He's right too: these lines are less polished than the previous episodes, partly no doubt because this is the first translation from Tonino's Italian original, and we've put in less time and work on refining it.

Fanny is very good in her jealous mode, and I like Peter's cool arrogance as well.

Unfortunately, we can't manage any more than that first set-up with the two cameras today. It gets dark so suddenly that we don't have a chance of going on to the next shot. It's really not enough for a full day's work, not even for Michelangelo. Maybe we can make up some ground tomorrow.

Wednesday 1.3.95   Forty-fourth day of shoot

Not much catching up today. We are able to complete the scene we began yesterday, but that's it. Once again we're filming with two cameras, and once again there's not enough light left in the afternoon for a second set-up. To begin with, both cameras are taking practically identical shots, then Fanny comes in view of camera two, which follows her across to the window, while camera one remains on Peter. After several takes, Michelangelo agrees to Aruna's suggestion to make Peter's shot a bit tighter, firstly because there's not much point in two roughly equivalent shots on two cameras, and secondly because it would take a close-up of Peter to answer yesterday's close-up of Fanny. For a long time Michelangelo opposes such a close-up, indicating that he doesn't need it, and only when we've almost given up hope does he ask Jörg on camera two to go in a bit closer. He makes a signal, pinching finger and thumb together: 'Stringere.' Whether that means 'open' or 'close' is something we have to guess each time.

Sometimes the framing does seem a bit random, and I wonder whether it is purely instinctive with Michelangelo, or whether he might be following some criteria that are not apparent to me. The rushes and his rough-cut tell me I was wrong to doubt him: they provide a thoroughly consistent picture. Probably it's just that Michelangelo's instincts and preferences are different from mine. However much I would endorse his long shots and his camera movements, I am equally passionately opposed to his use of the zoom and the extreme close-ups that are generally his only alternative.

When we have to stop for the day, very early, the producers look gloomy. In the last two days, we haven't even achieved what we were supposed to do in one.

'The day's loveliest moment occurs almost by accident': a kiss through glass between Weller and Ardant

Thursday 2.3.95 Forty-fifth day of shoot

Fanny's last day. We're filming the jealousy scene in the bathroom. Again Michelangelo uses two cameras, but today it's extremely effective. Because they're both facing the same way, there doesn't have to be any compromise over the lighting. The day's loveliest moment occurs almost by accident, but it's the kind of accident you have to deserve: when Roberto finds his wife in the shower where she's hiding from him, drunk, and kisses her through the glass wall of the cubicle, his own shadow falls across Patrizia's face, so that it looks as though he's kissing his own reflection

Fanny plays the drunk beautifully. Many actors just can't pull this off, but Fanny is believable.

Michelangelo directs the long 'jealousy' dialogue between Roberto and Patrizia in bed, with great lightness of touch and humour. He's really in his element in this kind of scene, and his

'He's really in his element . . .': Antonioni directs the bedroom spat between Ardant and Weller

instructions as to position, movement and gesture are all precise and spot-on.

To general astonishment, we're through very early today. As so often happens, we work much better under pressure – the producers had threatened dire consequences if we failed to finish in this location today.

The whole crew gives Fanny a rousing cheer.

I'm up all night over my screenplay. That, too, *has* to be finished by tomorrow!

FRIDAY 3.3.95 Forty-sixth day of shoot

For the last two days of the shoot we're in the Paris apartment of Olga, the lover.

Because of the preparations for my own shoot, I can't spend much time on set. I'm generally only present for the final run-through and the filming itself. The apartment is so small, we're all treading on each other's toes as it is.

Michelangelo shoots one set-up by the door with a single

Chiara Caselli as Olga – unmistakably an Antonioni female

camera – Roberto's arrival – and then a second shot in the sitting room: Roberto tries to tell Olga that it's finished, but she seduces him before he can say anything at all, and then he forgets what it was he came to tell her. Peter and Chiara are both extremely disciplined, and follow Michelangelo's occasional brief directions with great precision.

In the meantime, I'm hunting for a printer to print out my finished screenplay, but it seems the whole of Paris is using Apple. Then I remember seeing a Hewlett Packard in the Fondation Cartier, take a taxi down there, and find my luck's in. I'm relieved I can at last give copies of it to the production department and to Michelangelo.

Even though I've done everything I could to try and shorten it, it still seems too long. My main problem is that I can't really judge which scenes will make the most effective transitions between Michelangelo's episodes, so I've had to keep one or two alternatives just in case. Even so, my framework narrative is going to be a highwire act.

In the afternoon we have a surprise visitor: Henri Alekan is standing on the doorstep. He saw the lighting truck parked outside and has come to see who's filming, and what. Henri was my cameraman on *The State of Things* and *Wings of Desire*, for which I brought him out of retirement. He's now eighty-six, though God knows he doesn't look it. He greets Michelangelo, and once word has got out who this elderly gentleman is who's looking everything over with such obvious expertise – obviously thrilled to breathe the atmosphere of a film shoot again – everyone wants to come and shake his hand. He enjoys the attention. He remembers some of the technicians from having worked with them. Then he takes his leave, and is gone as suddenly as he came: a ray of sunshine on a dull day.

SATURDAY 4.3.95   Forty-seventh day of shoot

The last day in Paris, and Peter and Chiara's last day. We're shooting their jealousy argument, and the sudden, passionate reconciliation that ends it.

Both actors are surprised at how graphically Michelangelo wants to play the scene and how far he means to go. There is fierce resistance from Chiara before Michelangelo finally gets his way, and she consents to be stripped naked by Peter.

In the end, both are incredibly good throughout the battle of words, the physical tussle, and then the sexual resolution of their argument. Peter is brutal and violent, Chiara coarse and then very tender.

Michelangelo at his monitor is gleeful at having his love scene played the way he wanted it. I've seldom seen him so enthusiastic. He really is like the cat that got the cream.

One last round of stills, and then the fourth episode is completed. The crew will get a day off, and then back to Ferrara, where Michelangelo will shoot the missing scenes from his first episode, and where I will then embark on my framework. Before that, though, I have a recce to do in Aix.

In the late afternoon I call on Jeanne Moreau to discuss her

'The battle of words, the physical tussle, and then the sexual resolution': Weller and Caselli

scene with Marcello Mastroianni, against the backdrop of the Mont Sainte Victoire, and to choose a costume with her.

Then we pack our bags, and, following a working dinner with Uli Felsberg (the German co-producer), Donata and I, together with Thierry Flamand, our stage manager, drive down to Aix.

We arrive at two in the morning, dog tired.

SUNDAY 5.3.95   Rest day

Rest day for the crew, recce for us in Aix. In the morning, my cameraman Robby Müller is joining us. We find all we need: the stretch of railway that runs alongside the Mont Sainte Victoire, the place where our painter will make his Cézanne copy – Patrick Morrison, who's actually going to paint it, is coming in two days – plus the hotel for the final scene.

Donata has had bad earache for the last couple of days,

which is another reason why we didn't fly to Aix. In the morning I take her to the hospital's A and E department, where she has it syringed by the same doctor who treated my throat infection a couple of months ago.

We find time to visit Cézanne's studio outside Aix. We're far from being alone; in fact, we have to stand in line for a long time while busloads of reverential Japanese file through.

Monday 6.3.95

We go through all the locations once more with Thierry, our art director, and his assistant Denis, who will prepare everything here. Then the others get on a plane to Ferrara, and Donata and I set off by car.

We finally reach Ferrara at around two a.m.

Tuesday 7.3.95   Forty-eighth day of shoot

While Michelangelo is in Comacchio, re-shooting the walk under the arcades and the kiss scene with Ines Sastre and Kim Rossi-Stuart, we're in Ferrara looking for further locations for ourselves, so we can't be there for the shooting. From the point of view of continuity, Michelangelo could have done with a foggy or at least an overcast sort of day, but the sun's shining instead. They go ahead and film anyway, as we hear from the production office later. When the crew returns from Comacchio in the evening Michelangelo and Alfio seem reasonably pleased. The first part of the dialogue seems to have gone well.

Then Donata and I sit down with Enrica and Michelangelo to go over the script for my framework. The Antonionis, it turns out, have several strong objections. Michelangelo doesn't care for the children in the Schiffanoia Museum – he doesn't like children in films. The bit where Irene and Vincent pop up in the fresco – the theme of the 'lovers' – he either doesn't understand, or feels sceptical about. I explain how I imagine the scene. As we read on, other scenes encounter similar opposition.

At the end of the discussion there is an unambiguous 'no' to a motorbike scene involving a group of youths, a 'no' to the use of Michelangelo's final shot from the Ferrara episode on the screen of the cinema the 'director' goes to, and a 'no' to the transition from the Paris episode. In that episode, I wanted to have Carlo's wife 'Claire' make an appearance; till now we had only seen a photograph of her in Michelangelo's Paris episode, and heard her voice on the telephone. I wanted Claire to be driving around in a truck packed with all the furniture from the Paris apartment, and talking to Carlo for the last time on the phone – a scene we had heard, but not seen. Michelangelo doesn't want any dovetailing with his stories; my transitions are to be confined to the figure of the 'director' and his experiences.

I succeed in defending the children in the museum and the appearance of Irene and Vincent, but I take out all the other parts of the screenplay that Michelangelo objects to.

He does a sketch of the way he sees the whole thing: four squares for his episodes, with little lines between them for my transitions. I'm not sure whether he's understood the intention behind my text, which was at pains precisely to connect four separate episodes, to furnish links between them.

Afterwards, I'm rather left hanging. Those cuts leave the structure of my screenplay rather weak. What spirit there is now to sustain everything, I'm not really able to say. 'Solo', Michelangelo said repeatedly – meaning, I think, that I should content myself with John Malkovich, and let him carry the joins by himself. But if there are to be no encounters between the 'director' and Michelangelo's characters, his episodes would be left standing in a kind of vacuum. Which I guess is what he prefers.

We should have had this conversation earlier! That it didn't happen till today is partly my fault for finishing my part of the screenplay so late. But how could I have finished it any earlier? Previous versions, which Michelangelo had also read, never provoked reservations on such a scale.

The producers stay out of the debate. They're naturally all in favour of cuts, and I can't blame them for that. They know I could insist on retaining every word. Our agreement is clear: Michelangelo is responsible for his four episodes, and I for the framework. But, of course, I find it completely acceptable that the two of us should discuss it, and that Michelangelo should have an opinion on my section of the script. I worked on his, too. After all, the whole thing is supposed to be a film by the two of us. But whereas Michelangelo's aim is obviously to keep his four episodes separate, I'm trying to give the film some moments of completeness and coherence – that was one of the main reasons why I chose the actor who played Michelangelo's director in the Portofino episode to be 'my' director as well.

I've never regretted so much that Michelangelo can't express himself verbally. The discussion over the script kept running into areas where communication was impossible.

I go to bed tired and discouraged. My filming begins on Monday. That's how long I have to make my screenplay into something coherent once more.

Wednesday 8.3.95   Forty-ninth day of shoot

Our recce today takes us to the seaside. We find a house on the lagoon for the scene where Marcello Mastroianni is supposed to appear as a fisherman, then we look at Jamaica Beach for the strand scene, which would be the transition between the Ferrara and Portofino sections of the film. We return via Comacchio, and drop in briefly on the crew. Michelangelo is just filming his last shot for the day, then he'll have all he needs to be able to cut the sequence together.

All day I try to find some line to guide me through my framework. What purpose are my links to have? What kind of 'poetry' or 'reality' should I use in them? I feel dizzy at times, and worried sick. Donata is a great solace to me with her positive attitude and her faith in God, which I'm able to share from time to time. She tells me that I should stay calm and not try to press everything out of myself, rather let things come to me instead.

In the evening we go out for a meal with Alfio and Pino. Tomorrow their work will have been done, and they will leave us. If it hadn't been my intention from the start to work with Robby, I would happily have kept Alfio as my cameraman and Pino as his assistant. They're both such nice fellows, and they're a good team. But against that is my twenty-year association with Robby, in the course of which we've learned an enormous amount together. I trust the way he sets lights, and his sense of images and movement comes closer to my own than those of any other cameraman I've worked with. And because Robby on principle operates the camera himself, there's no job for Pino either.

In the evening Beatrice draws up a new shooting schedule, on the basis of a vague new list of scenes I more or less plucked out of the air. Today's recce has at least helped me to see the scenes more in terms of their locations. I can at least tell Beatrice *where* we're going to be shooting, and probably *how long for*, even though I'm still not sure *what* we'll be shooting in every case, *what* will be at the heart of my scenes, and *what* will hold them all together. But at least yesterday's panic is over.

Tomorrow is Michelangelo's last shooting day. Whatever I shoot on Monday has to come from the heart, and be straightforward. Be *easy*. I think I've hit upon a good new scene with Marcello. My script always contained a scene with a 'tired man' and a 'weeping woman' that I wasn't willing to give up, though I never found the right place for it. Now I have the notion that Marcello Mastroianni might play that part. He's going to appear in each one of my transitions in a different guise. So: what if the 'fisherman' and the 'tired man' were to be one and the same . . . then who would play the 'weeping woman' opposite Marcello?

Instead of using Michelangelo's last Ferrara shot of Silvano walking away, I'm going to try and use the end of *Il grido* in my cinema scene. And instead of the screenplay's transition from Paris to Aix using the character of Claire, I'll probably shoot a scene on a train with some anonymous female character. Everything will get a bit simpler. I think it was good advice of Enrica's, that I should trust my locations and find 'powerful settings'. I think I have them now for each scene.

Thursday 9.3.95   Fiftieth day of shoot

This is Michelangelo's last shooting day. There's only one shot to do, the repeat of a take that was probably scratched the first time round: having run off, Silvano comes back and knocks on Carmen's door, and she lets him in.

In contrast to the way he did it at first, Michelangelo shoots the scene as a master, and won't listen to Alfio's suggestion that he go in a bit. He shoots it again and again, with tiny variations, as though to put off the end for as long as possible.

But finally it's over. There is extended applause from the whole crew, and many people are in tears. Michelangelo's own cheeks are wet. It can't just be sorrow that the filming is over – there must be a measure of relief in it as well. Michelangelo has achieved something that, even a few months ago, no one would have thought possible. In spite of his age and his handicap, he has brought in this film he has been waiting twelve years to make! Apart from clocking up a couple of extra days, he's stuck to his shooting schedule and kept to his budget, and, as the months have passed, he has gained in confidence and mastery. Today's Michelangelo is nothing like the Michelangelo we encountered at the beginning of the shoot, back in November.

Enrica and Andrea stand either side of him, clapping as loudly as anyone. And yet the two of them deserve it quite as much as he does. The film couldn't have been made without them, and certainly not in such fine style. Enrica has represented Michelangelo quite magnificently, always backing up her husband through thick and thin. Andrea, his personal assistant, was always at his side too, supporting him as he walked, carrying his script for him, reading from it whenever he wanted, guessing his every wish, and serving him in the fullest sense of the word. If Andrea had not been around, there would have been hopeless confusion over all the different versions of the script in their various languages. Michelangelo always had his copy in Italian, the crew largely worked from the French, and a lot of the lines were spoken by the actors in English. Andrea's second task, as well as looking after Michelangelo, was to co-ordinate all the numerous script changes, and it was a task he fulfilled as selflessly and dependably as the first.

It's the last day for a lot of the crew as well, while for others it's the beginning. Robby and Christopher Porter, his gaffer, are already busy with the preparations, and aren't quite sure how to behave with the camera crew they've come to replace. I introduce Robby and Alfio to one another. They are both cordial enough, but a little sheepish. It can't be an easy matter for Alfio to hand over to Robby.

But my decision to go with Robby is the right one; I realize that with every conversation we have. The two of us have, as it were, 'grown up together'; we've been through so much together already, I'm sure we have a better chance of making this tricky 'framework' than I would have with Alfio. It's almost more of a personal than a professional judgement: no amount of craft or expertise could replace the trust that Robby and I have in one another, or the shared aesthetic that has evolved in the course of the ten films we've made together.

In the afternoon there is a long production meeting with all the heads of department. You can sense how much everyone is looking forward to the next couple of weeks, and the ones who have been with Michelangelo will welcome a change of tempo.

I'm still not sure of the exact running order of the scenes between the end of the Ferrara episode and the beginning of Portofino, but a new structure seems to be slowly emerging. I give Tonino a call, and he says he can be in Ferrara tomorrow evening. I'm delighted to be getting one more script meeting with him.

We hear that John Malkovich will be able to join us on Sunday and begin shooting on Monday, which is great news. That means the schedule will go as planned. Until today, it had looked as though John would only be arriving on Monday.

In the evening, we have a farewell party in a country restaurant for Michelangelo and everyone else whose work is now finished. One or two people make little speeches, and I too feel compelled to say a few words. It's difficult to know what to say to Michelangelo. There's a great distance between us, as there has been all along. Maybe it's a mutual fear of getting too close, and perhaps a certain feeling of rivalry too, though more on his side than mine. Or? It bothers me that I still don't really know where I am with him. What does he *really* think? Was he really grateful for my work, or was I just a necessary evil? He's been so blunt at times, I've had to wonder.

It's really hard to say goodbye to Alfio and Pino. Driving back to the hotel, I have to tell myself once again that it's only by going with Robby that I have any chance of putting my personal signature to my own parts of the film over these next couple of weeks, which are all I have.

Friday 10.3.95

I have a minor breakthrough today, working on my transition between Michelangelo's Ferrara and Portofino episodes. By dropping everything before the cinema scene, I've made it all flow much better. The Apollo cinema is an amazing location, too. I noticed it in the middle of the old city on my first visit to Ferrara: half 1920s cinema, half church (one of its two auditoriums is a deconsecrated Romanesque chapel).

I want my sections to be as light and surprising as I can make them. After all, they don't have to carry any sort of plot or message. Michelangelo's episodes speak for themselves, and the more affectionate and personal my transitions are, the better they will work.

The actors are arriving tomorrow. I'm really pleased to be seeing Irene, Vincent and John again: they gave 100 per cent for Michelangelo, and it was a pleasure working with them. And I'm so looking forward to seeing Marcello.

Discussions with Robby and Christopher, even on technical

matters, soon become discussions about content. It's a privilege to have a cameraman you can really talk to, not just about images, but about what's behind the images, what they should convey.

Lisbon Story is going on general release in Italy, and in the evening, between two screenings, there's a public discussion of the film in a cinema in Ferrara. Unfortunately, I'm rather tired and distracted, and the questions are largely uninteresting, so the whole thing is a slightly fruitless exercise.

Tonino gets in late in the evening, bringing with him not just his usual air of good humour, but a positive gale of optimism and joy. We agree to start work first thing tomorrow. I want him to tidy up some of the exchanges, and a couple of scenes need to be completely rewritten.

SATURDAY 11.3.95

Our last day of preparations. As always happens on such days, hardly anything gets done. A thousand people come to you with a thousand questions, and by the end of it you haven't really got anywhere at all with the ones that really matter, like: is there something else I can leave out? What can I cut? My sections probably still come to nearer thirty minutes than twenty. Tonino can't help either. But because no one can say what kind of transition would be effective, I don't want to drop anything at this stage that might turn out to be essential. I've only got two weeks anyway, and I want to make the most of them by shooting all I can.

In the afternoon Tonino and I have a public discussion with architecture students at the University of Ferrara. It seems irresponsible to take time off so soon before the start of shooting, but the production company promised it to the city, which has helped us in all kinds of different ways, and has also contributed financially to the filming here.

The huge hall is crammed to bursting point. The discussion begins a bit sluggishly, but then, thanks to Tonino's energy and the curiosity and open-mindedness of the students, an exciting conversation develops about cities, city planning, images and cinema. We leave with a sense of satisfaction that it's gone very well, and that we were able to give the students something worth having – which is probably unusual in these kinds of staged conversations.

Sunday 12.3.95

Pretty hectic all day. Even though it's supposed to be a rest day, every department is working flat out. The art department is toiling over the backdrop for the museum scene, and all the actors have costume and make-up trials.

But what I'll remember of today is this: how, suddenly, at dusk, Enrica, with Michelangelo on her arm, comes up to Donata and me and suggests that the four of us all go to a church and say a prayer together on the eve of the shoot, just as we did all those months ago in Assisi. That had been a somewhat improvised occasion, when we were driving to Portofino from the Antonionis' place in the country, and had stopped in Assisi to visit the cathedral of Saint Francis, who is important in the lives of both Enrica and Michelangelo. The five of us – Andrea was there too – found ourselves in the basilica together, and we all said a prayer for the upcoming shoot.

On Enrica's suggestion we decide to drive to a Carmelite cloister we once looked at in the course of a recce. By the time we find it, though, the cloister gates are locked, but after several rings a tiny window opens and the face of an old nun peeps out at us. Enrica explains what we're here for, but the nun declines: she can't let us in, it's their prayer hour. But we should go home in good heart, because the sisters will include us in their prayers.

On the way back to the hotel we pass Ferrara cathedral, just as the gates are closing. They don't want to let us in either – it's now closed to the public – but this time Enrica manages to get us in for five minutes. And so the five of us find ourselves once again sitting in a pew in an empty church, folding our hands and praying, each in our own way: Michelangelo with an ironical little smile, Donata deeply, Andrea devoutly, Enrica with eyes closed, and I rather worriedly. Michelangelo and I glance at each other briefly over the heads of the others, and he nods reassuringly: 'It'll be all right.'

Monday 13.3.95 Fifty-first day of shoot

Unfortunately Irene only has this one day for us, because tomorrow she's flying off to America. There's nothing for it, then, but to shoot all her Ferrara scenes today. So my shoot kicks off with a pretty screwed-up shooting schedule: as it's market-day in the town, we have to wait till afternoon before we can film in front of the castle. We can't therefore film chronologically and begin with the first shot of Irene coming out of the castle; we have to start at the end, with Irene and Vincent missing each other. She's sitting on a bus, he sees her go by and recognizes her, but too late. The bus drives off.

Robbie and I mapped out the bus scene last night, scribbling it down on a tablecloth in a pizzeria. It all looks slightly different, now that it's physically in front of us. Instead of a stationary beginning we go for a tracking shot: we expressly don't want to cut from the 'director's' eye to what he's supposed to be seeing. Instead, then, the camera leaves John, crosses to Irene, who's just sitting down, and stays on her until the bus stops and Vincent is seen standing directly outside the window, transfixed.

It feels wonderful to be working with Robby and Christopher again. And filming for myself, instead of having to watch, gives me such a buzz that I hardly know what to do with myself. I can't seem to stand still. Maybe the tracking shot in the moving bus is an expression of that. Even for Ennio, our experienced Italian key grip, that's a first.

Just as we're ready to go, Michelangelo comes up and surveys everything from his car. He doesn't want to get out or look inside the bus. He's busy preparing for a retrospective of his paintings in his native city, and after a while he drives off. Everyone waves as he goes. He seemed cheerful enough, especially the inimitable way he greeted me – finger and thumb pinched together, waving his arm up and down. I wonder what he meant this time? 'Good luck!' or 'Your turn now!' or 'How's it going?' or, more ironically, 'Don't fuck up . . .' or 'This better be good . . .' Who knows.

'Filming for myself . . . gives me such a buzz': Wenders gets back behind the bullhorn

I can't tell how the scenes I'm going to shoot today will sit with his first episode, which will follow on from it. I think it's best not to think about it too hard anyway, and use my instincts more. I'm sure I won't be doing Michelangelo's stories any favours if I try and film in his manner. Quite the opposite: the more I do things my own way, and the less my lead, the 'director', tries to 'be' Michelangelo, the better and the more effectively we'll lead up to and present his four episodes.

John looks a little different from the way he did in Portofino. We've cut his hair shorter and darkened it a bit, plus he's got a little three-day growth of beard, which makes him a bit rougher. I'm in two minds about his Burberry: any actor wearing that can't help but be associated with Humphrey Bogart. What the heck, though, I like John better like that than in the leather jacket he wore in Portofino. We tried out a few hats on him yesterday as well, but that was no good at all. Each one looked sillier than the last.

At the very last moment, we supplied Vincent with a wig. He looks good with long hair. A bit neglected, less cheerful. But I'm especially pleased with the way Irene looks: less of a country innocent, more like a young ballerina.

We finish the morning shoot almost on time, but then right at the end lose some time over a tracking shot that is unexpectedly problematic. First, the long shadow of a church tower creeps ever closer, reaching Vincent just as we're about to start. It would take us too long to re-lay the tracks, so we carry on in the shade. Then we try to build a little bridge over the tracks, so that a couple of extras can go by on bicycles once the camera's passed that point. That 'bridge-building exercise' takes time, and doesn't achieve anything in the end because the extras make a hash of it, and keep setting off too late to get in shot. After five or six takes I call a halt, with the annoying feeling that we'll probably end up using the very first take, before the sun had quite disappeared, after all. We've wasted an hour, working needlessly.

Then it's lunchtime and, as so often happens in Italy, the break goes on for half an hour longer than it's meant to, so afterwards we have to scramble to catch up.

The sun has almost disappeared by the time we're in position to shoot in front of the castle. The first shot with Irene and John works fine: she comes out of the castle and walks past him, he turns to take pictures of her as she goes. Then panic breaks out: the shadows are lengthening over the square, creating an almost instant discontinuity with the next shot. I ditch the planned tracking shot, and we start filming immediately, without a single rehearsal. For the next five minutes everyone's running around like crazy; even as the clapper falls, some last bits of equipment are being carried out of the picture! After two takes in rapid succession, the light is gone. The crew hasn't had to dash around like this for months, but it does us all good to work up a bit of a sweat.

Then there's another battle against the clock, to get Vincent's first appearance – another long tracking shot – with a reverse-zoom. (These two shots, Robby tells me, are the first we've ever done with a zoom. Must be Michelangelo's influence . . .)

There's just enough sunlight here, because we're on the other side of the castle.

Whew! On my first day, we barely get through what we had to do. The sun goes down seconds after the last clapper. I'm very satisfied.

TUESDAY 14.3.95 Fifty-second day of shoot

We begin our two-day shoot in the Schiffanoia Museum, in the hall with the famous fifteenth-century frescoes of the signs of the zodiac, the months and the seasons. A little boy comes running up the stairs, late for class. The teacher – Marcello's first day! – gives him a ticking off, and then goes on with the lesson. Malkovich comes into the hall shortly after the boy and starts taking pictures of the frescoes, thereby disrupting the class.

We're still working on the lighting when Michelangelo arrives at the museum. He walks up the big flight of stairs and takes a look at our set. He indicates to me that he hasn't been in this

Malkovich, snapping frescoes at the Schiffanoia Museum

room since he was a child, and then he walks up and down for a long time, studying the wall paintings. Then he sits down in a corner next to Marcello, who tells him a story, and the two of them burst out laughing. Photo op, of course! Everyone who has any kind of a camera charges over to their corner. They play along, strike poses and allow themselves to be thoroughly photographed – Michelangelo with the piratical smile he only ever produces for the camera.

Finally he gets up. Goodbye. He's going back to Rome today, and in a couple of days he's flying to New York, and then on to LA for the Oscars. He is visibly moved to be leaving us. He's not the only one to wipe away the odd tear. Then he disappears slowly down the stairs on Enrica's arm. We're on our own. Everyone feels the change, and for a while we're all rather quiet.

But then the lights are ready, and we embark on a highly productive day. By evening, we have an unbelievable forty shots in the bag; many of them are inserts, but it's still an impressive total. Once on *Hammett* I managed thirty-six in a day, and I thought that record would never be broken . . .

Working with Marcello is a delight. To begin with, he's still improvising his long and difficult text, but by the end he's letter-perfect. He really lives each take, and is totally believable as a teacher, devoted both to his class and his subject. He loves acting so much that if I fail to shout 'Cut!' at the end of his text, he carries on improvising until he has everyone in stitches. Once, when John Malkovich knocks over his pointer in the master-shot, and I don't call a halt when John has left shot, Marcello walks over to his pointer, picks it up, mutters 'Bloody tourists!' and various other things under his breath, and launches into a crazy lecture on God knows what.

John is no slouch, either, when it comes to ad-libbing. On one take, a little boy drops a crayon, and John picks it up and hands it back to him, before going over to the wall, and photographing details from the fresco. When he's taken his pictures on the last take, and his camera suddenly starts automatically rewinding – which of course is even more disruptive to the class than his picture-taking was – John incorporates that extra disturbance into his performance; his reactions are so funny that the shot may be ruined by the sound of the director helpless with laughter in the background!

The children play along attentively. When we're taking close-ups of each of them – to show while the frescoes come to life in their imaginations – I admire their wide, beautiful and already completely individual eyes. Michelangelo had taken great exception to this sequence in my screenplay, precisely because of the *bambini*. Now I'm glad I didn't give in to him, and insisted on having them in, in spite of his inevitable 'Via!' I'm convinced it will be an important and beautiful scene.

Finally, we do a series of shots without the children or the actors, just of the frescoes, all sorts of angles and formats, for the digital special effects that are planned for this scene. The two characters of the young man and the young woman are going to come to life, move, and finally leave the fresco behind. A dog is going to lift his head, a hand is going to call for attention, another hand is going to caress a child, and the young woman is going to lift her head to look at the young man. The teacher's lecture was all about their 'impossible love'. Later on, in the studio, we'll film Vincent and Irene in front of a blue screen, and then the computer will incorporate their images into the wall-painting, so that it won't be the actors beginning to move in the fresco, but real two-dimensional figures with scratches and stains and holes. Therefore every shot of the wall has to be exactly measured, so that we can film the actors in an identical manner, at exactly the same angle, distance, focal length and so on.

WEDNESDAY 15.3.95   Fifty-third day of shoot

Our last day in the Schiffanoia Museum. Another day with many, many camera positions, because we're filming lots of inserts of the children's drawings. Altogether, Aruna has calculated we have seventy-two shots in this sequence.

We finish late in the evening; dead tired, but with the sense of having shot a fine opening scene for the film, even though it won't be right at the beginning, because before that we have to have the 'director' flying in, driving through Ferrara in the fog, getting out, going for a walk, and encountering the boy who leads him up to the museum. All that follows – Irene and Vincent emerging from the frescoes into the city, missing each other, only to meet up again finally in Michelangelo's last episode – is based on this scene with the teacher, the children and the 'director'.

THURSDAY 16.3.95   Fifty-fourth day of shoot

The arrival of the 'director' in foggy Ferrara. I've been quietly dreading today because no one would or could tell me what the fog would actually be like. Everything depended on the weather, especially on the strength and direction of the wind on the particular day. We therefore tried to find narrow little streets for the scene, and finally came up with something close to ideal.

Our special effects crew from Marseilles do their job spectacularly well. By the very first take you can't see your hand in front of your face any more. Suddenly we're swathed in fog, blinded by it. Panic, then laughter. 'Hey, Dmitri, that was too much. Can you give us a bit *less* next time?'

My idea is that the first sketchy figures you make out in the fog are somehow difficult to place; you don't know what end of the century you are. This all depends on the quality of the fog, though. I quietly arranged the scene so that, if need be, I could cut into it later, without the historical ambiguity. But the fog looks splendid, to the naked eye anyway. We won't know until the rushes what the camera makes of it. All of us are coughing and spluttering in the smoke. I wonder whether the oil-based preparation is quite as harmless as the Marseilles boys assure us it is.

What then uses up a lot of time, as always, are the car mounts, inside and outside the car. It seems to take an eternity to get the camera securely bolted on to the bonnet, or two cameras inside in the back. We even went as far as getting hold of a second, identical Citroen, so we could get both cars rigged up at the same time. Just as well that John Malkovich is a first-class driver, and skilfully navigates the Citroen stuffed with cameras, lights and sound equipment through the fog. He even takes it back to the starting line after every shot.

In the end I'm satisfied with everything except a shot of a little boy who runs up, looks into the camera, and asks what time it is. (The camera, at that moment, is subjective, and takes on the role of the narrator.) The boy is supposed to look right into the lens. But he doesn't trust himself, and each time he looks up at John, who's standing next to the camera, holding his arm and wristwatch in front of it. Maybe, I think after a couple of takes, I should leave out this subjective camera bit. But it's too late – the shot and the track have been set up, and a further change would make it impossible to finish the rest of the day's programme. So I can't change anything, and have to try and work on the boy. But he keeps his inhibitions, and that subjective shot remains a thorn in my flesh till the end. I hope I won't regret it when I'm standing at the cutting table.

At the back of my mind, there's always that slight doubt whether what I'm shooting is really a good preparation for Michelangelo's first episode or not. Through the figure of the 'director', I've got rather hung up on the idea that all the episodes might emerge from photographs. The basis for that is a passage from Michelangelo's notebooks:

I only discovered reality when I began photographing it. Photographing and enlarging the surface of the things that were around me, I tried to discover what was behind them. I have done nothing else in my career.

Even if the philosophy behind that isn't mine, that little excerpt was a great help to me in finding a kind of animating principle for the director. Because otherwise, John's part would be rather notional, even though he fleshes it out and dresses it up with lots of little tics and gestures and, most of all, with his look.

I remember the other two films of mine where I had men taking pictures: Phillip Winter in *Alice in the Cities* and Ripley, alias Dennis Hopper, in *The American Friend*. John is cooler and more dispassionate about it than the other two men, but with each take the camera seems to be growing together with him more. I notice him holding it differently each time, even caressing it.

By the end of the day we're all coughing like mad. I'm relieved we've got the fog behind us now. What other terrors lie ahead? The beginning as such, with the 'director' in his plane, is still outstanding, and I can't help feeling that everything is still quite literally 'up in the air' and that I haven't yet dropped anchor anywhere. I hate being this 'fast and loose' with chronology, and swear for the thousandth time that I'm never going to do it again, however logical and sensible and useful in production terms, etc.

Friday 17.3.95   Fifty-fifth day of shoot

Another day with an enormous workload. In the morning we film the continuation from Michelangelo's first episode at the Palazzo Diamante: Silvano has left Carmen, and walks down the foggy street, while Carmen watches him from her window. Cut to the 'director', who's watching him go.

But how? It's a brilliantly clear and sunny day. There's no continuity with the milky light at the end of Michelangelo's final shot. We make a virtue of necessity: if it's not going to look the same, then let's make it radically different. John is standing on a balcony above a window which is identical to Carmen's, though it's actually on the other side of the building. The camera rides up to the empty window, on the very same crane that Michelangelo used, and then on up to the 'director', who's just taking a picture, though not of Silvano leaving, as the camera goes on to show, but of the empty, sunlit street. There follows, still without a cut, a vertiginous pan of 180 degrees back to the Palazzo Diamante, and the camera slides down it, to fade into the next shot, which will have John just stepping out on to the street. The crane shot is really difficult for our key grip Ennio, who from the day he began has been given ever trickier assignments. On top of that he has a temperature, probably brought on by that wretched chemical fog yesterday. At any rate, we lose a lot of time, and by the time we're moving on to the next set-up, the minutes are ticking by and the sun is creeping slowly up the wall of the Palazzo Diamante. On the last day of preparations, Robby and I noted the precise moment when that wall looked its most plastic, when it simply *had* to be filmed. Now we're about to miss it, if only by a few minutes. By the time the camera's on the rails – which I've cut in half to save time – it's almost too late. So we start filming in a total panic, without any rehearsal for camera, crane or actor. And we do succeed in catching the dying rays of sun on the wall, but everything else goes awry: Robby gets his pan wrong at the end, the extras come running on at the wrong moment, and the crane goes up when we really didn't want it to. It's enough to make you cry, but then again, it's really so comprehensively botched, you have to laugh. Jacques Tati would have been proud of that shot.

Now that we've lost our race against the sun, we stop and catch our breath, and then finish the scene in more orderly fashion, even if there's no real continuity with the last shot. I'm glad I had the foresight to do one take in shadow, when the sun was briefly obscured by clouds. I have a feeling that's the version we're going to end up with at the cutting table.

In all probability the end of the shot will have to be dropped, too. Because the proportions of the Palazzo Diamante are so vast (like so much else in Ferrara – no wonder de Chirico painted here!), I ended up posting a couple of giants next to the huge gate, and having a dwarf come out of them. The 'giants' are a couple of basketball players from Bologna, the 'dwarf' the friendly night porter in our hotel. John is just walking past the big guys, when the little fellow walks out of the gate. At that point I always made the camera go up, and it wasn't till lunchtime – when it was much too late – that I realized I shouldn't have done that at all, because that cancels out the difference in height. I should have kept the camera pointed *down*. Oh well, next time I'm filming with dwarves and giants, I'll know better.

So, as we make our way to the next location, I'm feeling rather ambivalent about the first part of the day. The next sequence had better turn out well. Two bungled scenes in one day is more than my self-confidence can take. Normally I wouldn't make these kinds of mistakes, I tell myself. The shoot came about after a lot of waiting, but still before I was really ready for it, and the jumbled sequence of the shots left me with no chance of establishing a rhythm. I hope I find one in the next two weeks.

The second sequence of the day is round the Apollo cinema. John walks past an old church which, on closer inspection, actually turns out to be a cinema. Someone is just leaving it by the back exit, and the 'director' takes the opportunity to slip inside. Once there, he realizes he's not alone – there's someone else in there with him. Then he also leaves, because he can't get his mobile phone to work in there, and John is all on his own. The exit door by the side of the screen has been left open, and the bulk of the scene shows the 'director' following the film on the screen, and another film, far more beautiful and gripping, which Life is putting on for him just outside the door.

Last night, on impulse, I rang Nicoletta Bracchi, who, just as impulsively, accepted my invitation. She is the 'star' of the film that is happening on the street, just beyond the screen.

It's not until we're both on set that we have a chance to discuss the scene. I suggest to Nicoletta that she appear in the doorway three times: once in daylight, once at dusk, and the third time at night. Each time, she's to call out something to her boyfriend, who lives in one of the surrounding houses, and have some sort of shouted conversation with him, unaware of the fact that she's being watched. We refer to her invisible friend in his attic apartment as 'Remigio'. Maybe Roberto Benigni can be persuaded to play the 'voice-off'.

We light and prepare the scene. In the meantime Nicoletta is sitting in a corner, writing her script. After a while, she comes to me with suggestions for her three appearances: first time, she asks Remigio to go for a walk with her, but he doesn't feel like going out; the second time, she offers to buy him dinner, but once again, he's not tempted; on her third visit, she asks if he'd like to sleep with her, 'Without a condom!' even, but nothing, it seems, will get Remigio to come down the stairs.

These three scenes come garnished with all sorts of little vignettes that happen outside the door, some of them spur-of-the-moment things, others that we've planned for a day or two: a pair of lovers, a couple arguing, a tired couple, children, bicyclists, dogs, a forgetful man, etc. By and by, a veritable catalogue of images from the Italian cinema passes by the open door beside the screen. Even though we're all exhausted, everyone gets into the spirit of this little film-within-a-film. People come forward with ideas for things to include. Henri, our props man, builds a huge pole, and carries that through the shot. A wailing baby is found, and time and again, our man with the mobile.

We film all that from inside the cinema, using two cameras, one of them trained on the open doorway and beyond, and the other wider, taking in the bottom of the screen as well, and John in the auditorium. In order to get everything in focus, John in the foreground and the streets in the background, we make use of a split-focus lens. That was something Robby and I used a couple of times in *Paris, Texas*. The trick is to align the split with a line that runs through the picture – otherwise you would notice the device.

The last shot of the day, and of the scene, is filmed way past midnight. Everyone has been up for sixteen hours or more, but no one seems tired. John gets up and leaves the cinema. The camera starts off inside, it retreats ahead of John, and once on the outside it opens into a big, high, wide shot in which you finally recognize that the cinema is really an old church. In the background Nicoletta slips away, still waving at the unseen Remigio, who probably shoots back a last intemperate reply, seeing as John looks up in his direction at the end.

The scene has turned into a completely self-contained thing, a kind of microcosm – much too long, of course, and only the feeling that it might therefore not fit into the film makes me unhappy as I fall asleep.

SATURDAY 18.3.95   Fifty-sixth day of shoot

To ensure that everyone will get their full ten hours off, we can't begin shooting till this afternoon. But today's schedule is fairly light anyway. We're shooting the immediate transition between my prologue to Michelangelo's first episode, under the arcades in Comacchio.

A feeling of *déjà vu* – not surprising, as it's the fourth or fifth time we've filmed in this location. But for all that, there are still new perspectives to be won in this unique street. First of all, in the afternoon light, we shoot John Malkovich getting off the bus, walking towards the arcade, and taking a photograph of it: that photograph will turn into the opening shot in Michelangelo's episode, of Carmen on her bicycle, emerging from the fog. It's a clear and sunny day, no hint of fog, and with a lot of effort and the use of our fog machine, we can just about produce a light haze. But maybe it really doesn't matter; maybe the discontinuities of light between Michelangelo's footage and mine are a good thing.

After that, we film up on the water tower, from where you have a great view of Comacchio and the surrounding countryside. The 'director' looks down on the locations for his story, and then slowly descends the spiral staircase. The shots we take here may be my most 'Antonionesque', but even as we're filming them I have a sneaking suspicion that they won't make the cut, and that my framework won't be able to contain any descriptive elements like that. We'll see.

In the twilight we take our final shot of the arcades, for the moment 'two years later' in Michelangelo's story when the narrator returns and speaks. Just putting John Malkovich in the principal locations of the story seems to be about the least obtrusive device I can use. In my screenplay I had come up with a different transition, but Michelangelo objected to it, so out it went. While we're filming this replacement scene, I can't help thinking that the original version – for which there's no time now, because we're leaving tomorrow – would have been much more useful to the overall flow, and that it was a mistake on my part to agree to lose it. My heart feels a little heavy. But there's no time to mourn these kind of things. I've invited the whole crew to dinner, and we all go to the 'Sole' restaurant in Porto Garibaldi. It's the first time I have all the actors together, because today Eva Mattes arrived. She has her one and only shooting day on Monday, as Marcello's daughter.

SUNDAY 19.3.95   Rest day

A so-called rest day, inevitably completely taken up with preparations for the week ahead. We see the rushes: Robby and I are generally pleased with the look of these first images.

In the evening I spend a couple of hours editing with Lucian Segura on a portable digital editing machine. There's a video projector in the hotel room too, so we can see the cuts on the wall, and not just on the little monitor. Our goal is to have a rough-cut ready as soon as the shoot's over, so I can take it to my editor Peter Przygodda right away. But that may not be possible, because already it seems very difficult to get early video versions of our footage, complete with soundtrack. The communications between production, lab, video duplication and sound-recording in Paris seems like a mare's nest. Kafka.

In spite of that, we can try out a few cuts, even if every other shot is either 'silent' or missing.

MONDAY 20.3.95   Fifty-seventh day of shoot

We drive out bright and early to Jamaica Beach, a location we discovered with Tonino first time around. It must be packed in summer, but it's all boarded up now. The swings are creaking in

Malkovich in the 'greyish marine light' of Jamaica Beach

the wind, sand has blown over all the terraces, and only the artificial palm trees are unaffected by the seasons.

When we arrive the place is bathed in the kind of greyish marine light I'd hoped for, but we're unable to film in it, and have to stand around for an hour. The trucks with the equipment either set out too late or they've got lost. When we finally unpack the cameras and lay tracks, it's beginning to spot with rain. But we don't let that put us off, and the first few shots are quickly in the bag. Malkovich arrives at the deserted café, goes inside, finds a postcard lying next to the telephone, goes back on to the beach, and sits on a swing, looking at the postcard. It's of a fishing village on the Italian Riviera, Portofino in fact, and that postcard will fade straight into Michelangelo's second episode. The picture on it is almost identical to the wide shot of Michelangelo's that opens 'La ragazza, il delitto'.

Just as we start filming John on the swing, the wind gets up and makes things very difficult. The calm morning sea is whipped up, all the fishing boats return to port, and you can hardly stand up without getting blown away. But the wind has its 'silver lining' too, and because we're sufficiently alert and quick on our feet, we can turn it to our advantage: the way the loose sand is blown along the beach, inches above the ground, makes it look like running water in a long exposure. For our scene, and the little time-gap in it, we could hardly have wished for anything better. We get several shots of the blowing sand, then the wind dies down again, leaving the beach swept bare.

We film a scene with Marcello and Eva Mattes, an echo of

their first scene – which we're only going to get to in the late afternoon. This is where they see each other again, after their parting. They play father and daughter, both of them very emotional and believable. The wind is howling around them; Marcello's cap flies off during every take and his false beard threatens to unpeel. Originally I'd thought of having the daughter played by Marcello's real daughter, Chiara, but she wasn't able to make it. But even she couldn't have done any better than Eva. We're all blue with cold, but boisterous and happy when we sit down to lunch in a restaurant on the beach.

The restaurant has a lot of pictures of actors on the walls, among them an old and yellowed one that the landlord draws our attention to. It's Marcello in his younger years, kneeling in the dirt – a scene from his very first film, which, he recalls, was filmed somewhere around here. In the background you can just about make out the fellow who wrote the screenplay, a skinny young chap by the name of Guerra – Tonino, or something like that.

In the afternoon we film the preceding scene, outside a fisherman's house on the lagoon. I had noticed the house on our first drive around the area, without ever guessing I'd come back to film in it. Once again we waste a lot of time with the car mounts, getting a shot of John as he drives up to the house. After that, we're up against the clock – the days are still short – and we need to rush to get through the rest of the schedule: another eight shots in all. We film as quickly as we can, never more than two or three takes: John climbing out of his car, walking out on to a spit of land opposite the house, and taking pictures of it from there. Just at that moment, as though summoned by his camera, two people – the fisherman and his daughter – come out of the house. They start having an argument. The young woman is carrying a suitcase and is obviously leaving; the older man is trying to keep her from going. The 'director' is too far away to be able to follow what's going on, let alone hear any of the words that are being exchanged. But when he takes a picture of them from a distance, the frozen image turns into the scene, and the father and daughter come closer and closer, as though, with the help of his camera, the 'director' had thought his way into the scene.

Then the girl climbs into the 'director's' car – no doubt mistaking it for the taxi she'd ordered – father and daughter exchange a few last words, and by now both are in tears. Suddenly there's the sound of a car horn, and the real taxi comes to a stop behind the Citroen. The girl sees she's made a mistake, and gets into the taxi, while her father apologizes to the solitary observer on the other side of the little bay: 'Scusi . . .' And cut. By the time we get to the most important part of the scene, the dialogue and the close-ups of Marcello and Eva by the car, the light's almost gone. (And how often that happens: because of shooting in sequence, or for various production reasons, the most important shots can't get done until it's practically too late!) But Robby manages to light the close-up of Marcello, and shoots it against the darkening sky. It's completely dark for the countershot of Eva in the taxi, but never mind. As it's a narrow frame and depth, Robby is able to light it artificially.

And with that we've managed a full and difficult day's schedule, under ideal conditions finally – the wind in the morning and the sunset in the afternoon. If it had been the other way round – the way the producers were urging yesterday – we probably wouldn't have got anything. We were lucky.

We wouldn't have been able to go on tomorrow in any case: the plane that's taking us to Marseilles, which we're going to film in as well, couldn't have been put off. Hiring a Boeing is no small matter. And so tomorrow we have another race against the clock. We've booked the plane for three hours; every extra hour will cost a small fortune.

If I can believe the producers – and I don't see why I shouldn't – we're almost out of money. I mustn't slip up on any of my twelve days, or incur any delays if I can help it.

We say goodbye to those members of the crew who aren't coming to France with us, among them the excellent Ennio, who hasn't been quite the same since the shoot in the fog and has been battling with flu ever since. He's struggled on manfully, but he can't do it any more. You can tell how galled he is at not being able to stay with us till the end. We still don't know who's going to replace him. The key grip is one of the most important people on a film set, just after the cameraman and the gaffer.

Tuesday 21.3.95 Fifty-eighth day of shoot

Driving to Bologna airport in the morning, we have a sinking feeling: there's not a cloud on the horizon. The pilot has no better news for us either – the forecast for the whole area is unbroken sunshine. So we can't film anything at all, because the opening scene on the plane wouldn't make any sense without clouds. After all, the film is called *Par delà des Nuages*, which means 'beyond the clouds'. (The title does nothing for me. It's vague, unpoetic, and only works in French, if then.)

We start off by flying the crew and extras to Marseilles. En route we set up the cameras: one at the front for the shots with Malkovich, and one at the back for his subjective views out of the window. I sit in the cockpit for a while, explaining to the pilot what we're doing, and how I want him to fly if we do manage to find some clouds. Apparently there are some far away in the Alps, around the Matterhorn. We land in Marseilles, let everyone out who's not needed for the immediate filming, and, on the suggestion of the flight control tower, set off towards Lyons, where we turn east and soon hit a thick layer of clouds.

The pilot cuts the altitude until we're gliding just above the clouds, and then we start filming. The plane banks steeply a couple of times – it's absolutely terrifying. A few of the actors and technicians look so green, they could use a bit of make-up. We bounce around in the clouds for a while, and knowing that there are a couple of mountains in the area doesn't make it any easier. But after half an hour the whole thing is in the bag, with some beautiful shafts of light streaming into the plane that we would never have been able to film so realistically on the ground, let alone in the studio.

We fly back, and, just before overtime kicks in, we're back on the ground in Marseilles. There, the Boeing 757 is rolled into a hangar, and we shoot one last take from outside, of Malkovich at the window leaning forward to look out. Stacks of clouds blow by. Our fog-crew is in action again. We all cough for a while and guzzle oil fumes, and then the first part of the film is done. It's a relief to have got to the beginning, and 'earthed' everything I've shot so far. Only now do I feel that Michelangelo's film is really getting a frame. For the first time, I feel we're on course.

WEDNESDAY 22.3.95 Fifty-ninth day of shoot

After cars and planes, today it's the turn of the train. In the course of the many 'road movies' we've made together, Robby and I have acquired a certain expertise in filming on various types of conveyance. Trains were never a problem for us. On the contrary, I always thought there was a kind of affinity between the camera and the train anyway, as both are inventions from the mechanical era. A train compartment with a window, I always think, is like a kind of six-seater cinema.

We film the beginning of the transition from Michelangelo's Paris episode to his fourth and last in Aix. During our recce last month we came across a disused bit of railway line that runs parallel to the Mont Sainte Victoire, and a little south of it. The stretch of line has been reactivated for our film, and we have been given our 'own' train, an electric locomotive with four passenger coaches. Just next to the tracks there's a smooth, straight road, ideal for our camera car. First we film a parallel tracking shot of the train, beginning with a couple who are wrestling on the edge of the tracks, and come rolling down the embankment. We have to shoot out of sequence again, so the scene before, where the woman tries to hurl herself under the wheels and the man prevents her, comes next.

Our two stuntpeople are very good, and thankfully clever enough not to be too slick about it, so it doesn't look at all 'like in the movies', but more of an awkward scuffle – very realistic.

The problem we have isn't with them, but with the train driver, who steadfastly refuses to go more than 20 mph. It's so slow that both our tracking shot and even the actual fight seem completely undramatic. Finally we get him up to about 30 mph, but that's as fast as he'll go. It still seems very slow, but I have to make the best of it.

Then we go on to the actual stunt, with two cameras. The star of the scene, and of the whole day really, is the mountain in the background. After the scenes with the train, we're going to continue with a Sunday painter who's painting the Mont Sainte Victoire in the style of Cézanne. Then, from his painting on its easel we're going to fade to a shot of the real Cézanne painting in the hotel in Aix, where our 'director' is just checking in.

Today Malkovich isn't required to do anything except sit on the train, look out at the view, make jottings in a notebook, and listen to a young woman who comes into his compartment and opens her heart to him. Before doing that, though, she answers a call on her mobile phone with the words: 'Don't look for me.' That's the actual transition to Michelangelo's third episode, which has that line in it a couple of times, both spoken on the phone, and both by a woman who's left her husband. That's to identify Malkovich as the person who's making up the story.

Sophie Semin, who's playing opposite Malkovich today, is another woman who's running away from her husband, and doesn't want him to find her. Sophie's a little nervous to begin with, and not quite sure of her lines, so we start with a close-up of John. That turns out to have been a stroke of luck, because right at the beginning of the first take this beautiful freak of light falls right across his face, and it stays there till we've ended the shot.

By now Sophie's got her confidence up, and she plays it beautifully. Because the compartment has mirrors over all the seats, it's very tricky to keep the lights, boom, camera, sound assistant and director out of shot. Everything is reflected two or three times. In the end I have to take a worm's eye view of proceedings, lying flat out on the floor, while the sound assistant is dangling up on the luggage rack.

We finish just before sunset, but on Sophie's insistence, we do one more take of her whole scene. (Later that will turn out to be providential, because all her other takes are scratched at the lab, and are unusable. The only one to make it into the editing suite is that extra shot – which we did 'as a favour' to her – because it was on a separate reel of film.)

Jeanne Moreau arrives in the evening. I go out to dinner with her and Marcello. They've known each other practically for ever, since Michelangelo's film *La Notte*, when they were real-life lovers. It's fascinating to hear them reminisce together, and I'm only sorry I can't record their conversation for posterity. Forgetful as I am, most of it has gone already. It's a sad fact that I only have a good visual memory.

THURSDAY 23.3.95   Sixtieth day of shoot

The main thing today is the scene with the Sunday painter, and his picture of the Mont Sainte Victoire, which is in the milky distance in front of him. Marcello Mastroianni plays the painter, in his third incarnation after the teacher and the fisherman.

Our location is a hill close to the town of Gardanne, from where there is a panoramic view across a valley and a plain to the mountain. Cézanne painted several of his pictures of Mont Sainte Victoire from here or somewhere very close to here. What drew me to the place, though, was the huge factory in the foreground, with its cooling towers and belching chimneys, which some time interposed itself between the place and the mountain. Patrick Morrison, my Irish painter friend, has done several pictures of it from here in the last couple of weeks, and we've chosen two of them: one in clear sunshine, the other in slightly hazy, late evening sun.

We're up on the hill in the early morning, shooting the scene between the painter and a critical passer-by, who complains

'Jeanne and Marcello were both wonderfully relaxed and funny': the lovers of *La Notte* reunited on screen

about how everything is copied nowadays, from paintings to dresses to rucksacks and watches, and God knows what else. Wouldn't a photograph be better than a Cézanne copy? The painter replies that he finds more satisfaction in retracing the gestures of a great painter than just going through his own pathetic, amateurish repertoire. Then he dips his brush in the paint and applies a dab of red to a twig near the top of the canvas. The camera pulls back, and dissolves to the identical dab of red in the actual Cézanne hanging in the hotel lobby. But that's the next scene. For now, we're still on the hill, and beginning to feel a little dissatisfied with the scene we've just done. Jeanne and Marcello were both wonderfully relaxed and funny, but the *light* wasn't all that I'd hoped for, or indeed what I'd seen here on previous visits. Today, there was always that milky haze coming between us and the mountain – which, after all, was our third character. It seemed rather hopeless to wait around for 'the light to change': nothing would happen till late afternoon. But then, an inspiration from Beatrice: we can return to the hotel, film Jeanne's part in the lobby, and then go back to the hill

165

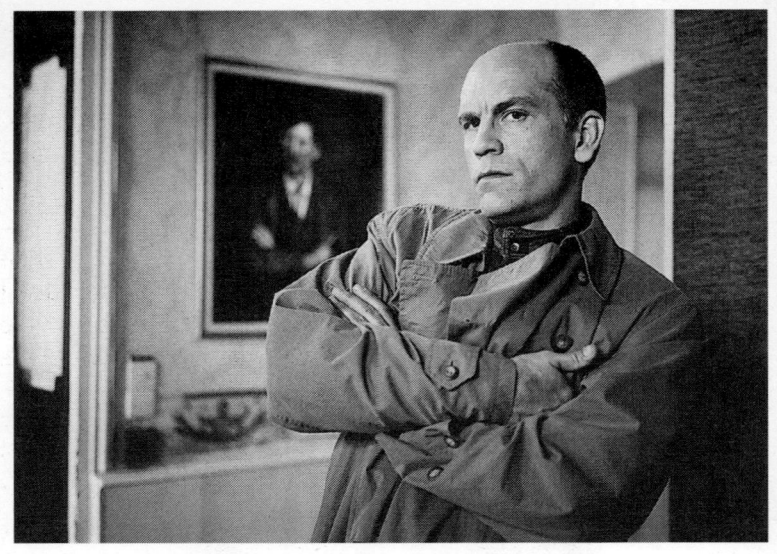

'Man with Folded Arms' – and John Malkovich.

afterwards. The rails and the little crane can stay where they are.

And that's what happens. After lunch, the whole bang shoot rolls back into town. We set up the lights in the hotel lobby. The camera pans back slowly from the Cézanne on the wall to show most of the room, and discover Jeanne, who's sitting in an armchair reading a book – Doris Lessing's autobiography – and watching John, who moves from the landscape of Mont Sainte Victoire to another Cézanne, 'Man with Folded Arms', and then tries to strike the same pose. She intervenes, and gives the 'director' little tips on how to be more like the painting: fold his arms the other way, head to the side, a more serious expression. John takes her 'direction' utterly seriously, but is so funny about it at the same time that there are probably a few more of my giggles that will have to be taken off the soundtrack. The time flies by, and we've just done the establishing shot and a close-up of Jeanne, when our scout rings in from the hill to say that the light is clearer now, and it would be worth trying again. Because we've done all Jeanne's scenes, and John is going to be filming in front of the hotel tomorrow in any case, we decide to break off the scene, pack everything up, and 'head for the hills' again.

With all our equipment, we get there just in time to retake the four shots that make up the scene, only this time using the other painting of Patrick's, with the hazy evening atmosphere. The light *is* better, if not as beautiful as I remember it the first evening I stood here. Jeanne and Marcello are really enjoying themselves, and from the point of view of the acting, the scene is better than it was in the morning. Because the sun is in the opposite side of the sky we have to reverse all the set-ups, so that the actors have the low sun in their faces instead of standing in front of it. We wouldn't have been able to boost the light anyway, as we left the generator behind in Aix. But even back to front the scene is good, if a little confusing to us. In the last five minutes before the sun goes down we even manage one extra shot, a wide shot showing both actors with the entire landscape spread out before them.

Then we take everything down. Robby and I ask ourselves whether we've ever filmed two versions of the same scene, one after another like that; if we have, we can't think of it. We did something of the sort in *Kings of the Road*, but that was for insurance reasons, and the two shoots were not on the same day.

In the early evening Jeanne says goodbye, because she has to catch the first plane back to Paris tomorrow. Today was the only day she could have filmed for us. To the whole crew her presence here was a gift.

FRIDAY 24.3.95   Sixty-first day of shoot

Tonight we shoot the last shot in the film: after Niccolo walks off into the rain at the end of Michelangelo's fourth episode, our 'director' watches him go, and then turns to go back inside his own hotel.

Before that, we have to film the rest of the scene in the hotel lobby: the countershot of John, and his walk out of the hotel on to the street, from where he observes Niccolo and the girl, which gives us our transition into the last episode: 'Questo corpo di fango'. Not difficult shots really, but for some reason we have trouble with them today, and they take an age to do. We all get in one other's way. Maybe it's because we've laid the tracks across the entrance to the hotel, and everyone going in and out trips over them. In the end we take twice as much time as we are allowed, and it's only in the late afternoon that we get to the final shot, the real task for the day.

And that *is* difficult. We've laid down a twenty-yard length of track, widely spread in the narrow Rue Cardinale, on which we have a heavy dolly with a gigantic crane on it that is going to extend to forty feet. The camera is attached to the end of the crane, and is fully manoeuvrable in all directions by a hothead. Generally, these kind of things have a gear attachment that the cameraman uses as a remote-control, but this one here is like a regulation camera, only instead of looking through the camera, Robby is looking at a video monitor. His movements are relayed via computer to the camera so that he controls it from the ground, but in exactly the same way as if he was in mid-air. As it climbs from three feet to about thirty feet, the crane, of course, makes a flexing movement, and we need to compensate for that by an equivalent, opposite movement along the track. In addition, the five stops that the crane makes *en route* all need to be measured with absolute precision, to within a centimetre. First, the camera follows the 'director' as he watches Niccolo go, before disappearing inside the hotel entrance. Then it rides up to the first floor, and peers into a room where a woman is singing her baby to sleep. Then across to the next room, where a couple are having sex. Then up again to a balcony on the next floor, where a woman is standing, smoking a cigarette, then goes back into her room to write a letter. And finally the camera moves to the next window along and sees John, just stepping over to the window, and looking out into the night. And all without a cut.

Understandably, the preparations for this scene go on for several hours. Each of the four rooms has its own little scene to direct and rehearse. The decor is adjusted, and then they are all lit. At the same time the entire street needs to be lit as far as the church. The rain machine is set up, so that it's raining as hard as it was in Michelangelo's last shot, and as the camera rises in front of the hotel, a little rain is sprinkled in front of it too.

I watch the goings-on for a while from a big ladder, from where I can see into all four rooms, as well as down the street. If this was a film about a film, it would look just like what I see in front of me. I'm reminded of Truffaut's *Day for Night*. The whole crew is working at the same time, on all their various tasks, which never happens in the usual course of things. Generally in films, things are done consecutively. But today everything is simultaneous: the stagehands keep rehearsing the complicated crane movements, the special effects guys are tinkering with their rain machine, the streetlights are covered with gelatine, there's an electrician at work in every room, Robby is hovering in six places at once, measuring the lights, Thierry Flamand is replacing the hotel sign, which broke earlier on in the evening, furniture is being carted around, make-up applied, hair combed, costumes altered. I don't think I've ever seen so much going on on a set at the same time.

At about midnight, we're finally ready to go. The shot takes three minutes, and there are so many ways it can go wrong that we're on take five or six before we even get as far as John – all the other takes were aborted before this point. You can't film two takes in quick succession either, because each one needs a reel to itself, so the camera needs to be reloaded each time. It's a thoroughly nerve-racking business. But because it *is* so difficult, and because everyone has to work flat out, the crew is completely focused all the way through, even though it's the second time in a row we've found ourselves working for a sixteen-hour stretch.

The twelfth take is the first one on which everything seemed to work. The crane movement is perfect and the actors are precise – all except for little Chan in the first room, who no longer needs to be sung to sleep, because he already *is* asleep.

Because it's already half past two, and it will take us a couple of hours to strike everything, I decide to call a halt, and just trust in our one good take. No further insurance, it's a wrap. Champagne all round, because we've finished in Aix, and this is John's last day. Tomorrow he's off to London to do a re-shoot for Stephen Frears's *Mary Reilly*. Huge applause for him, and then everyone, actors included, help strike the set.

Dead tired, but very happy, we fall into bed some time in the not-so-small hours.

Saturday 25.3.95

We have to travel up from Marseilles to Paris at noon. Air Inter's on strike, though, and we sit around for hours in Marseilles airport. We could have done with a few more hours of sleep instead!

In Paris at last, but too late for a recce at the Roissy 2 airport. We have to go straight to the hotel, where there are a dozen actors waiting for us. Almost at the end of our shoot, we still need to cast some of the mini-scenes we're shooting in our last two days: meetings between men and women that happen as though seen and photographed by our 'director'. Since we've established the idea of him taking pictures, these freeze frames are an attempt to keep him in the film, even though physically John Malkovich has gone.

In the evening there's an advance screening of Benigni's film *Il mostro* in the Champs Elysées. We go along to say hi to Roberto, and also to take a break from the shoot for a little while. I haven't seen a film for ages. Having gone from *Lisbon Story* straight on to Michelangelo's film, I don't think I've been inside a cinema in almost a year.

The monster is so funny at times, I laugh tears.

Sunday 26.3.95 Rest day

Rest day, or, more accurately, preparation day for the final recce in Roissy. We take a look at the newly completed TGV station there. What an incredible location! I could happily make an entire film here; the only problem is where to pitch the camera, what to leave out. There are too many interesting and exciting possibilities. The building site outside it is a thrilling place too: an enormous motorway junction with a huge excavation and thousands of cranes, with planes taking off and landing on every side, and an occasional express train appearing underneath them. Very close to the runways there are underground lines that haven't been roofed in yet. A phenomenal scene.

And over it a sky like that in a Flemish painting. The air is clear; every detail, every colour is sharply etched. I take pictures like a maniac, and hope we'll be able to capture a bit of all that action tomorrow.

Monday 27.3.95 Sixty-second day of shoot

Marcello's last day. We have an early start and drive out to the airport, to yesterday's futuristic terrain. But today's it's bucketing down. I'm forced to rethink all the shots I'd planned yesterday. There isn't a hope of us doing anything like it today. In fact, it looks as though we'll have to film indoors with Marcello. He has to leave for Genoa in the early afternoon, and it won't have stopped raining by then.

Marcello, today, is in his fourth incarnation in the film – as a bewildered and confused businessman, offering his philosophy to a (hardly) waiting world. He has a difficult and comic speech on the significance of the North Star as the new fixed point. Today, we take things in order: first, we discover him on one of the travelators, walking up and down, haranguing his suitcase. Then he comes out into the departure hall and sidles up to the microphone at the information desk to broadcast his message. And finally we come across him on the platform, waiting for a train, mumbling the rest of his credo to himself. Marcello is magnificent as this hopeless crank.

Lunch is in a tent in a carpark. It's so windy by now that the tent is almost blown apart. After a while it starts hailing, and then snowing.

So we carry on indoors, with two of the mini-scenes that we were casting only two days ago. Rüdiger Vogler appears in one of them, again as a travelling businessman. He's sitting in the departure lounge talking on his mobile phone, back to back with a woman who's also talking on hers. The two of them stand up at once and collide with each other, so that their mobiles get entangled. It's not an easy scene to do, because it requires split-second choreography from the actors. In the end we get it to work, though. Rüdiger has a real gift for this kind of thing. He does a new variation on each take. I'm glad to have got him a brief appearance in the film. (Reckoning them up, after *Goalie, Scarlet Letter, Alice, False Movement, Kings of the Road, Till the End of the World, Faraway, Arisha* and *Lisbon Story*, this is the tenth movie we've worked on together.)

Then on to the second mini-scene: a man and a woman meet at the luggage carousel over their two identical-looking suitcases. I've never worked with the actors before. It's not easy, therefore, to keep the scene short and sweet. I really think that's the hardest thing for me. At the same time, I like the challenge. I see it as a kind of five-finger exercise for the comedy I want to do soon, where every single shot has to be just so, not even a tenth of a second over. That Benigni film we watched yesterday was a good example of how timing really is the essence of good comedy.

In the end we do get to film one shot outside, in the building site I was so smitten with yesterday. A lost father runs around carrying a couple of suitcases, and his wife and child find him. There's a brief splash of sunshine, just enough for a couple of takes. Five minutes later, blizzard conditions descend once more.

Tonight, Michelangelo picks up his Oscar in Hollywood. The

hotel where we're staying, the Golden Tulip, doesn't have Canal Plus, so we can't watch the ceremony – or at least not live, at four-thirty in the morning . . .

TUESDAY 28.3.95
Sixty-third and penultimate day of shoot

Another instance of *déjà vu*: we find ourselves filming outside the Hotel Lutetia, where we stayed during Michelangelo's Paris shoot. So we treat ourselves to breakfast in the Brasserie where he filmed the opening scene of that episode.

There's only a skeleton crew with me today. We have two more little scenes to shoot, two more encounters between a man and a woman. Two German friends of mine, Antonia and Bernard, appear in the first one. A woman comes running out of the Metro, her plastic bag tears, and its contents spill across the entire street. A helpful passer-by bends down to help her pick things up. At first she wants to decline his help, but when she quickly looks at him, she recognizes him as someone she hasn't seen since her childhood. The two of them slowly straighten up and fall into one another's arms . . .

That's all. Does it go on for too long? It's hard to cut it down to a couple of seconds, and it seems mean to the actors. Still, I try to keep it as short as I can. When it comes to the editing, it'll be useful to have the phantom 'director' taking a photo of it. That way, I can freeze the scene whenever I want, and we can go forward from there.

The second scene is based on Robert Doisneau's celebrated photograph of the couple kissing in the middle of a crowded street in Paris. The photograph looks like a snapshot, though I gather he set it up and used actors. In our scene, we have a woman jumping out of a taxi, running over to a man who's waiting at the edge of the pavement, and tapping him on the shoulder. He turns round in surprise, recognizes her, and they fall into a passionate kiss, just like in the Doisneau photograph. Agate, a young actress whom Michelangelo was going to cast as the secretary in 'Due telefaxi', gets to play this little part by way of consolation. And seeing as she's going out with Fabrizio, our set designer, he gets to play the man. I don't want to make him jealous of some other guy . . .

Then I drive to the airport and catch a plane to Munich. Tonight is the premiere of a short film I made with the students at the film school there, on the invention of cinema in Germany by the Skladanowsky brothers: it's called *Meself, the Daughter or How we Invented the Flicks*.

Again, when we set up this date a long time ago, it never occurred to me that we'd still be filming, much less that I'd have to fly off to be there on the eve of the last day! But I really couldn't do it to the students to cancel at the last minute.

The whole thing is quite a strain: the flight, the film, a public discussion with Werner Herzog, dinner afterwards . . .

Still, I enjoy the conversation with Werner, and I'm really fond of the little film, which I've not seen before on a big screen. The music seems a bit galumphing, though. I think we should re-record it with fewer players; maybe later, when we do a sequel. But that's really the least of my worries.

I wish I could have stayed with my crew in Paris.

WEDNESDAY 29.3.95   Sixty-fourth day of shoot

The last day.

My shoot ends on the day all the newspapers are carrying photographs of Michelangelo with Jack Nicholson. They're all full of reports of Oscar night, and I buy all the newspapers I can lay my hands on, especially the Italian ones.

But it's another few hours before I'm in Paris, feeling completely shattered. Having got up at five o'clock and made my way through a blizzard to Munich airport, I find that it's closed to all flights, and I have to sit and wait. What if this unimportant jaunt makes me miss the last day of the shoot? Esther Walz, our costume designer, is in the same boat as me, and she's just as tense. She too had a premiere to attend last night in Munich, and now has to get back to Paris. Irene Jacob and Vincent Perez both need to appear in historical costumes today.

It's almost midday when we arrive at the Eclair lab, where the crew is waiting to see rushes of yesterday's make-up tests. Vincent has come out looking red and rather effeminate, while Irene appears strangely aged by her make-up. We discuss the necessary adjustments before dashing off to the studio in Neuilly where we're doing our last bit of filming.

We're filming in front of a big blue screen. The computer plays our footage of the frescoes in the Schiffanoia Museum on to a monitor, and we have to try to fit in the actors as precisely as we can, so they can then be digitally 'painted in'.

Our first subject, though, is a greyhound with whom we're trying to do exactly the same thing. In terms of his colour, and the shape of his head, he's a perfect fit, but that's about it. We cannot get him to take up the same position as his painted ancestor to save our lives. We shoot three large ten-minute rolls, before we have – with luck – enough footage for him to lift his head in the fresco for three seconds.

Then we carry on with Vincent, who looks less effeminate now, thank God, than in the screen test, and in fact looks really handsome in his Renaissance garb. When we get to the point and map his face on to the face of the unknown fifteenth-century man, the effect is eerie: his eyes fit the shape exactly, his costume is perfect, even his hair is exactly the same as that of the man in the fresco. Then suddenly the painting can move, and we can guess what the end result will look like, once the surface detail of the fresco is 'transplanted' on to Vincent's skin.

We shoot Vincent's movements in four different frame sizes. Then we film a hand: in the fresco, there's a woman tenderly holding her hand over a baby's head – well, now she's going to get a chance to touch it.

Irene, too, has been beautifully matched to her predecessor, almost better than Vincent because there's less face to be seen on the fresco, only the eyes, really, and the brow. When the eyes move for the first time, when the woman blinks, and turns to look at the young man – who's been waiting for her to do just that for hundreds of years – it's a thrilling moment. I had dreamed it might be like this, but the 'reality' of it is quite breathtaking. There wouldn't have been a way of getting that effect with traditional film technology; it needed to be done digitally, on a computer. It's the first time I've used this sort of equipment in a film. I've only been able to experiment with this on some commercials.

In Irene's case, we shoot five different frame sizes. Then, when I see the pictures of the man and the woman together for the first time on the computer, I'm disappointed. I must have made a mistake in the framing: either I left the man too high up in the shot or I put the woman too far down. She took up a lower position under her archway, and I framed her in relation to that, instead of framing the figures relative to each other. Even with simple things like filming motionless figures on a fresco, you need to watch yourself. I wasn't thinking in the museum of having to cut from one figure to the other and back – I just tried to take optimal pictures of each figure for itself, and that was my mistake. I hope it won't be as serious in the edit as it seems to me now.

When Irene is finished, we do a few more close-ups of hands in various positions. One beckons, one raises an admonitory index finger, one reaches out and shakes another hand.

And that's it. Not quite nine o'clock, considerably earlier than the producers expected after my late arrival this morning.

My first thanks are due to Robby and Donata. As the evening goes on, with all of us eating at a buffet in a hall off the studio, it gradually sinks in that this adventure is over for the moment. There's still the editing and the post-production to come, but they can't be as risky or as onerous as the shooting.

Someone turns up the music, and we dance ourselves off our feet.

I fall into bed, exhausted. I dream that Jeanne Moreau wants to come out of the painting too, but for some reason I can't do it for her. I know I'll be dreaming of the filming for weeks to come; I always do when I've finished a shoot. And they're always dreams where something impossible has to be done, too. I've never been on a shoot where I haven't been plagued by these nightmares afterwards.

Epilogue

Beginning of June 1995

Michelangelo has edited his episodes in Rome; in fact he's been finished for a couple of weeks. I did my preliminary editing electronically, and the fine editing in Berlin with my old friend and cutter Peter Przygodda. To keep my 'narrative frame' under thirty minutes I had to leave out one long scene in its entirety, namely the scene in the Apollo cinema. I remain very fond of it; it's probably the best thing I've filmed this time out, and certainly it's the most relaxed and the most charming, but it came to eight minutes, and its mood probably wouldn't go very well with Michelangelo's rather serious and sometimes melancholy stories. I know from past experience how it's sometimes best *not* to use one's favourite scenes. At thirty minutes I'm near the upper limit of what we agreed on. Michelangelo's sections come to around 100 minutes at the moment, so our combined length is well over two hours. The producers have stated that they want the film to come in at under two hours. Something will have to go.

Our respective parts are assembled in Rome, and on 3 June we see them run together for the first time. There are very few people present: apart from Michelangelo, Enrica and Andrea, there's only the Italian editing crew, Tonino Guerra and myself.

The atmosphere is quite tense, and no one wants to say much in advance. Then we see the film for the first time. I know my sections by heart, Michelangelo likewise. I've seen rough-cuts of some of his episodes, but he's edited them further, so I know there's probably the odd surprise in store for me. Michelangelo is seeing my framework for the first time. I'm not sure how well he remembers my screenplay.

He watches it all attentively, without any perceptible reaction except during the long final crane-shot in front of the hotel in Aix, where he suddenly feels moved to angry protest: 'Niente!' I think he had it in his mind that his own final shot, of Vincent's departure, was going to be the final shot in the film, and was therefore disturbed to find that it carried on after that.

Afterwards, I explain to him that you can't have a framing narrative if that narrative doesn't close. There is no further discussion at this point, but we decide to go through the film again tomorrow at the editing table.

The following day we spend a couple of hours in the editing suite, but all we talk about is the music. Enrica told me some time ago that Michelangelo was thinking about using rock songs for some of it, and I made up a few cassettes for him, of all kinds of different things. He liked Van Morrison best, and he wants to use a couple of his pieces on the Portofino episode – instrumental pieces, though, nothing of Van singing.

Lucio Dalla is going to provide the music for the Ferrara episode. The opening music, and music for the Paris episode, are both still to be decided. I suggest Laurent Petitgand as a composer. Maybe U2, who are just now in the studio with Brian Eno, will also come up with something.

We barely mention the film edit. It will obviously take Michelangelo a bit longer to get into the film that's now been pieced together for the first time. We decide to get a flash print made, so that Michelangelo can try out a few cuts. I understand that he wants to study the whole thing at leisure at the cutting table, and then offer me his editing suggestions when he's finished. So I'll have to come back in a week or so.

I accept one spontaneous suggestion of Michelangelo's without any discussion: the two little scenes that we filmed in Paris right at the end, with the two couples, that then get freeze-framed into a photograph, really seemed to bug him, and I agree right away that they can go.

Before I leave, I remind Michelangelo that at the beginning of our collaboration we had agreed we would each be responsible for our final cut, but that I would still be interested to hear any suggestions he might have when we next met. He would have to understand though, that the final decision remained with me, and, of course, vice versa.

As I fly home in the evening, I'm a little unsure whether he still feels himself bound by that, or whether he perhaps thinks he will have the final say over the entire film. If that's the case there will certainly be fireworks at our next meeting, because I have one or two suggestions to make to him myself. The 'sex scene' with Peter and Chiara needs shortening, I think. It begins well enough, but it goes on and on, and is finally insufferable, close to pornography.

A week later I'm back in Rome. In the editing suite you can cut the tension with a knife. Claudio, Michelangelo's editor, gives me a whispered warning: Michelangelo has cut a lot.

And so he has. He's taken all the freeze frames out of the introductory scene. The 'director' doesn't take pictures any more. He doesn't meet the boy who takes him up to the museum. The museum scene itself is cut by half. The two 'lovers' don't emerge from the wall painting any more, and there's much less of the children. After the museum, the group of scenes around Vincent and Irene are gone: the two of them coming out of the castle, the scene with the bus, where they miss each other, etc. The next thing is the 'director' turning up under the arcades. The transition to Michelangelo's first episode is the same.

When I look across enquiringly at Michelangelo, he looks at me sadly and points to himself: 'Ferrara'. It seems he doesn't want his city in my part of the film. It's his terrain. 'Get the message, won't you, this is my story, and my film!'

In the transition from his Ferrara episode to the second story in Paris, he's left out the first scene with the 'director' in front of the Palazzo Diamante, and the whole of Marcello's scene with Eva Mattes. I'm pretty shocked, but manage not to say anything. I want to get to the end first. Between Portofino and his third episode in Paris he's left out Marcello's scene in the airport, though that wouldn't have made much sense without his previous appearance as the fisherman. And I had already agreed to lose the little short scenes that followed that. Between Paris and the fourth episode in Aix, he's completely re-edited my train journey, cutting out the man and woman fighting on the embankment, and the appearance of the elegant lady. The scene with Jeanne Moreau and Marcello as the painter has also gone, but the transition to the hotel is still there. He's left my final scene, though, the crane-shot in front of the hotel up to John Malkovich looking out of the window.

End of show. Silence. Michelangelo looks over to me and shrugs. He liked it better that way, he says. And he looks at me so sadly, it's as though it's his episodes that have just been butchered rather than mine. I'm in a state of shock, but I still can't help smiling wryly at him.

I need air, and I need to think, so I go for a walk round the block. There's not much left of my framework. My leitmotif – the 'director' going around taking his pictures, from which the stories are supposed to develop – doesn't really exist any more. Marcello, intended as another source of continuity in the action, makes little sense now. So what's left? And what am I to do? Insist on my right to my own final cut, and disregard Michelangelo's suggestions? Not since *Hammett* have I allowed anyone else to cut or edit anything I've filmed. That's part of the reason why I became my own producer, so that this kind of thing wouldn't happen to me again. But there's no sense in just being disgruntled. I need to give Michelangelo an answer. What is it that's really happened?

In his proposed edit, Michelangelo has spoken to me quite unambiguously, and has said something like this: 'Leave my film alone! My stories don't need any framing, they can stand by themselves.' What he wasn't capable of saying in words, he's just told me in the form of his edit.

Then why did I devote the last couple of years to this adventure with Michelangelo? So that we could be antagonists now? Wasn't it my desire from the start to help him prove that he was still able to make a film, *his* film, maybe his last film?

I go round the block one more time. Then I tell Michelangelo that I understand what he's saying to me, and I want to take his edit back to Berlin with me, and think about it.

Back in Berlin I spend a couple more days with Peter Przygodda, re-editing my framework. We follow some suggestions of Michelangelo's, and completely re-edit other bits. I shorten my contribution by more than half. I can't leave the museum scene in its present mangled condition, so I have no choice but to take it out entirely. That all but removes Marcello from the film, and I have to take out his wonderful airport scenes, which don't make sense any more. Only the section with him and Jeanne would still work, out of context, and I re-insert that as the only surviving scene of what we did together.

It's difficult, not surprisingly, to explain this radical surgery to Marcello. Initially he's furious and says that he'd rather not appear in the film at all, if he's only got one scene left. I can't say I can blame him; on the contrary, I'm just as disappointed myself.

When I'm really past hoping, Marcello returns, and in a splendid gesture towards Jeanne Moreau in particular, he allows me to include their scene together after all. I will always be grateful to him for his magnanimity. I don't know what I would have done if I'd had to lose that scene as well. Maybe I would have taken myself off the entire project. *Grazie*, Marcello. You are indeed the lovely man I always sensed behind the wonderful actor.

We re-edit the train scene. The film is now twenty minutes shorter, because we have a couple of cuts to suggest to Michelangelo as well. The result is a different film, really, perhaps a better one. My narrative frame has a different function, but one that I can stand by in its economy and restraint.

The next screening in Rome, in the presence of the producers, goes smoothly. Michelangelo accepts my 'abbreviated version' in its entirety, including our suggestions as to his parts.

Four weeks later, we're mixing. Two pieces by Louis Petitgand, two by Lucio Dalla, two by Van Morrison, and two by U2 are included in the film.

Another three weeks, and the film has its premiere on 3 September 1995 in Venice. It really is Michelangelo's film. He's fought for it tooth and nail and against all odds. He's done wonders in the process. It's a moment he's had to wait twelve years for. There is lengthy applause, but no amount of clapping could do justice to what he and Enrica have achieved.

I do not regret I accompanied Michelangelo through this time.